# CHANGING PATTERNS OF AUTHORITY AND LEADERSHIP

DEVELOPMENTS IN THE ROMAN CATHOLIC CHURCH IN
ZIMBABWE AFTER VATICAN II (1965–1985)

*Paul Henry Gundani*

UNIVERSITY OF
ZIMBABWE
Publications

All rights reserved. No part of this book may be reproduced in any form or by electronic or mechanical means, including information storage and retrieval systems, without permission in writing from the publisher, except by a reviewer, who may quote brief passages in a review.

© Paul Henry Gundani, 2001

First published in 2001 by
**University of Zimbabwe Publications**
P. O. Box MP 203
Mount Pleasant
Harare
Zimbabwe

ISBN-13: 978-0-908307-82-1

# CONTENTS

List of Abbreviations ................................................................. v
Place Names ........................................................................... vi
Acknowledgements ................................................................. vii
Introduction ............................................................................. 1

## Part 1: Towards The Era of the 'Local Church'

CHAPTER 1: A New Emphasis in Ecclesiology ...................... 11

CHAPTER 2: Translating Vatican II into Practice in Zimbabwe . 17

CHAPTER 3: Church Renewal and Challenges from the Minority Regime: ............................................... 29

CHAPTER 4: The 'Local Church' and Local Political Mobilisation ......................................................... 45

## Part II: The 'Local Church' and Social Justice

CHAPTER 5: New Institutional Means to Pursue old Priorities in the 'Local Church' ........................ 69

CHAPTER 6: A New Means of Catholic Service: The Justice and Peace Commission (1972–80) .................. 75

CHAPTER 7: The Justice and Peace Commission in Independent Zimbabwe (1980–85) ................ 101

CHAPTER 8: Reflections ....................................................... 131

Sources ................................................................................ 137

Index .................................................................................... 147

# LIST OF ABBREVIATIONS

| | |
|---|---|
| AGM | Annual General Meeting |
| CA | Catholic Association |
| CADEC | Catholic Development Commission |
| CAFOD | Catholic Fund for Overseas Development |
| CAU | Catholic Development Commission |
| CCJP | Catholic Commission for Justice and Peace |
| CIIR | Catholic Institute for International Relations |
| CMRS | Conference of Major Religious Superiors |
| CPS | Precious Blood Sisters |
| CSSD | Commission for Social Service and Development |
| CSsR | Redemptorist Fathers |
| DIOC | Diocesan Clergy |
| DCLA | Diocesan Council for the Lay Apostolate |
| FMS | Fraternity of Marist Brothers |
| GTCA | Gokomere Training Centre Archives |
| HAA | Harare Archdiocesan Archives |
| NAH | The National Archives (Harare) |
| HOD | Heads of Denominations |
| IDAF | International Defence Aid Fund |
| JA | The Jesuit Archives |
| JPA | Justice and Peace Archives |
| JPC | Justice and Peace Commission |
| LCBL | Little Children of Our Blessed Lady |
| LCM | Little Company of Mary |
| NADC | National Association of Diocesan Clergy |
| OFM | Order of Friars Minor |
| OP | Order of Preachers |
| RCBC | Rhodesia Catholic Bishops' Conference |

| | |
|---|---|
| RCCL | Roman Catholic Council for the Laity |
| RSHM | Religious of the Sacred Heart of Mary |
| SJ | Society of Jesus |
| SMB | Swiss Foreign Missionary Society of Bethlehem |
| SMI | Spanish Missionary Institute |
| SPB | St Paul Brothers |
| UDI | Unilateral Declaration of Independence |
| ZANU | Zimbabwe African National Union |
| ZAPU | Zimbabwe African Peoples Union |
| ZCBC | Zimbabwe Catholic Bishops' Council |

# PLACE NAMES

**PRE-INDEPENDENCE**
Gwelo
Marandellas
Salisbury
Sinoia
Umtali
Wankie

**POST-INDEPENDENCE**
Gweru
Marondera
Harare
Chinhoyi
Mutare
Hwange

# ACKNOWLEDGEMENTS

I am grateful to all those who facilitated this study, first when I embarked on a Doctor of Philosophy degree at the University of Zimbabwe. Special thanks go to my Chief academic supervisor, Professor M F C Bourdillon and associate supervisor, Dr Ambrose Moyo. Professor Carl F Hallencreutz and Fr Albert Plangger provided valuable insights and editorial advice and encouragement on how I could transform what was an academic thesis into a readable book. To all those who encouraged me along the way, whose names are not mentioned, I say thank you. Finally may gratitude and admiration go to the rural and urban missionaries, local priests and sisters, and lay Catholics who shared with me their insights and faith.

## Introduction

# Scholarly Interest in Zimbabwean Catholicism

The Roman Catholic Church, which is numerically the strongest individual religious movement in Zimbabwe[1] has attracted a lot of interest from various scholars and students alike. This interest has been illustrated in the studies by Dachs, A J and Rea, W F (1979), Linden, I (1980), Maxwell, D J (1986), McLaughlin, J (1996), Randolph, R (1985), Turner, A (1978) among others. Some of their works, both books and unpublished theses, focus on the Church's participation in the transition from colonial Rhodesia to independent Zimbabwe.[2] Others, however, focus on how the Church's missions functioned as a means of popular mobilisation during the liberation struggle.[3]

These works and others of a more general nature provide a solid launching pad for an in-depth study of the actual process of transformation within the Roman Catholic Church. They also attempt to show how power was shared or transferred within the institution, and what this means to the Church's participation in the continued transformation of post-independent Zimbabwe. This study aims to probe into the actual changes of the Church's structures, ethos and power relationships.

I have been profoundly challenged by Ian Linden's and Sr Janice McLaughlin's works which have succeeded in laying a foundation that any other history on the Roman Catholic Church in Zimbabwe has to take account of. However, the two authors have certainly not said the last words. As G R Elton aptly asserts, 'The whole of history — the whole of a person, a period, or a problem — can never be got between the covers of one book ...'[4]

Ian Linden's *The Catholic Church and the Struggle for Zimbabwe*, ably tackles the Church's political involvement during the colonial era as well as during the armed struggle for independence. In his analysis, Linden argues that the Church in Rhodesia consisted of two different churches going in different directions. On the one hand, there was the 'teaching church' of the hierarchy and the urban clergy, while on the other hand, there was the 'listening church' of the rural missions and local parishioners. The former, Linden argues, preached an otiose Gospel, while the latter identified with, and fulfilled the aspirations of the poor.[5] Linden manages to construct a very partisan history in favour of the 'listening church'. His stated concern is 'to risk telling the truth in the hope of genuine reconciliation'.

It is not surprising that Ian Linden, as a member of the Catholic Institute for International Relations (CIIR), an organisation that published the dossiers of the Commission for Justice and Peace in Rhodesia, glorifies the role played by the Catholic Commission for Justice and Peace in the history of the Church and society at large. His self-assurance, in spite of dependence on very few people that he shared ideological perspectives with, leads him to the one-sided picture that he produces. Consequently, his book is overly critical of the 'teaching church', that in fact formed the Commission that he lauds.

This study builds on Linden's analysis in areas like education, justice and peace. Moreover, we will tackle some issues that Linden referred to in passing, like the Catholic African Association (CAA). These are areas that further highlight the complex change that the Church underwent, over the years.

Sr Janice McLaughlin, documented in great detail the war experiences of four rural missions, namely, St Albert's, Avilla, St. Paul's Musami and Mutero. These missions, she argues, were part of the greater rural church and were open to radical changes. This change resulted in what she calls the 'People's church', which contributed to the liberation struggle by way of offering 'relief and development aid, logistic support and legitimation for guerrillas, human rights advocacy, theological reflection and mediation or conflict resolution'.

McLaughlin's case studies add to those by Ranger and by Bourdillon and Gundani, and in a way provides a balance to David Lan's findings on the war of liberation. Through her case studies, McLaughlin shows that there existed a high level of cooperation between the rural church and the nationalistic guerrilla forces.

This study not only highlights developments within the rural church: it also explains the advocacy role that the Catholic Commission for Justice and Peace played during the struggle for independence, which is the *terminus ad quem* for her study. Thus it also traces the Commission's role in formulating programmes of education for the grassroots communities. Furthermore, the study examines the extent to which the Commission operated within the parameters and ethos of the local church, which strove to be self-supporting. The question of local support and its implications in terms of power relationships between the clergy and the laity is thus a major concern of this study.

Any discussion on the Commission for Justice and Peace would not be complete without drawing upon the invaluable material provided by Diana Auret in her book *Reaching for Justice* (1992). Auret details how for over two decades, from 1972 to 1992, the Commission became the 'voice of the voiceless'. What Auret fails to show, in her rather triumphalist study, however, is how the voiceless have become empowered by the Commission to the extent that they now can cooperate with, rather than continue to depend on it. R H Randolph, who served the Bishops' Conference on its secretarial staff from 1970 up to 1982, and having, before that, been instrumental in bringing before them the serious implications of the 1969 constitution of Rhodesia, also contributed significantly to the writing of the history of the Church. In three books, *Church and State in Rhodesia* (1971), *Report to Rome* (1978) and *Dawn in Zimbabwe* (1985), Randolph presents a history from the point of view of the official church. In spite of his partisan approach, his books contain a wealth of information on the Church of the seventies. Having served as the secretary of the Catholic Bishops' Conference, his concern for the official perspective however leaves many gaps in the process of the transformation within the Church, which surely got its impetus from both internal and external forces at work at the grassroots levels.

*The Catholic Church and Zimbabwe* (1979), written to mark the centenary of Catholic endeavours in Zimbabwe, examines the ever-changing response of the 'teaching church' to the local situation. It highlights the process of indigenisation through African vocations and leadership as well as ritual and liturgy. The two authors, like Randolph, also present an official if not self-censored history. The book chronicles the events that took place in the one hundred years that it studies without much time to discuss the causal elements behind those events.

## Aims and objectives of this study

This study explores the transition within the Roman Catholic Church, from a predominantly Missionary-led religious movement in the mid-1960's to a local Church where the missionary, the indigenous clergy and laity shared responsibilities from the grass-roots level up to the top hierarchy in the mid 1980's. The study therefore aims to:
- identify directions and dynamics in the process of transformation motivated by Vatican II by examining the changes that took place in the relationships between the national administrative structures of the Church and their local constituencies, and
- critically assess the policies and programmes of the Catholic Church in Zimbabwe, after the Second Vatican Council, in its attempt to transfer 'power'[12] from missionaries and the white elite to the indigenous clergy and the black laity. We will also have to relate these internal church developments to external factors, which affected church life in the transition from colonial rule to independence in Zimbabwe.

## Sources, problems and limitations

This study draws primarily upon sources found in Church archives, which include the Jesuit archives, the Archdiocese of Harare archives and the archives of the Zimbabwe Catholic Bishops' Conference. Other archives consulted were at Mambo Press (Gweru) and at the Gokomere Training Centre for the laity, outside Masvingo town.

The archives of the Jesuit Fathers proved to be very helpful as I was allowed full access to the well sorted and catalogued material without being given only the files that the archivist thought contained the information I wanted. Gokomere Training Centre's archives also proved to be very informative, though not always well arranged in boxes according to subject. Rev. Dr T Jakata gave me the liberty to peruse through file after file without restriction. The material that I have found particularly relevant to this study had to do with the apostolate of the laity and the National Association for Diocesan Clergy.

While I was not, for understandable reasons, really left to read through files of the Catholic Bishops' Conference, the assistance I got from Bishop P. Mutume was tremendous. The files that he pulled out for me on liturgical developments in the Church were highly informative.

The archivist at Mambo Press gave me all the *Moto* magazine issues that he had from 1980 to 1985. Although I did not get much from them for this particular study, I have found them very useful as background material.

I was lucky to stumble into the Rhodesia Catholic Bishops Conference newsletters at the time that the Jesuit Archives were about to throw them away for lack of space. Fr Pat Lewis donated almost all the issues from August 1970 up to 1985 for use in this study. These have been very valuable on the subjects of justice and peace. I also found assistance at the archives of the Archdiocese of Harare where there were some files on the laity which included activities of the Catholic African Association.

The JPC newsletters proved tremendously valuable for an understanding of the operations of the Commission from 1972 up to 1985. Mr Nicholas Ndebele gave me, for personal perusal, a whole collection of issues that the Commission's archives had more than one copy of. Sr Janice McLaughlin added to the material on the JPC by giving me photocopies of the material on the Commission that she had obtained from various sources and in her personal archives.

Knowing people who mattered like Bishop P Mutume, Brother L Fischer, and Rev Dr T Jakata, proved to be an asset. Their recommendations were very important for my archival researches and thus I have relied on oral sources as well. My interviews often filled the many gaps that were left by written sources. Throughout this study I have tried to maintain a close relationship between written archival documents and oral interviews. From reading the documents I got a clear picture of the prospective interviewees and vice versa. The people who were referred to in the documents as involved often became my first targets for interviews. I would follow them up at parishes, if they were lay members but used the current Catholic directory to locate members of the clergy. This sometimes meant travelling long distances to interview some of my resource persons. In most cases I managed to find the people I wanted to interview. Many of them, both clergy and lay, cooperated and were pleased to share what they knew on the subject that I wanted to explore.

In the majority of cases, I interviewed people as individuals but in some cases, there was so much enthusiasm exuded by many parishioners that I would decide to have group interviews. This I did at St Peter's Mbare, Tafara, Harare and Mt St Mary's, Wedza. Group interviews save time and one is able to quickly get the general picture on a parish and the members' consensual opinion on some issues such as justice and peace, and the role of the laity in decision-making. The major disadvantage of the group method, however, was that people tended to skirt around controversial issues unless I was aware of them or referred to them myself. In a group, individuals would not want the whole church to know that they disagreed with the pastor or the leadership on certain issues. However, in very few cases, members of some parishes, who knew that there was consensus against the parish priest or a sister on some issue, would ask me to take up the issue with the bishop or sometimes emphasised that I had to publish it. Such information was in most cases difficult to ascertain from the clergy's point of view.

Otherwise, sensitive information was in most cases given by individuals. However, this often happened only when I promised to keep the identity of the interviewees anonymous. This applied to both the laity and junior clergy, who did not want to be put on record for fear of victimisation.

## Methodology and interpretative perspective

This study is restricted to the Roman Catholic Church in Zimbabwe and in this book, the term 'Church' will refer to the Catholic Church. When the word church appears with a small c, it is used in the context of parish or the small Christian community. In very few cases, mention is made of some ecumenical cooperation or consultations. However, Chapters 3 and 4 discuss issues related to education and small Christian communities which have wider ecumenical implications.

This study ventures a historical/chronological examination of the process of change that occurred in the Catholic Church in Zimbabwe from the end of the Second Vatican Council (1965) up to 1985. As already stated, primary archival sources and interviews from both clergy/religious and lay people, will be the major sources of information. I will relate my findings to the literature that I have already referred to in my review section whenever this is considered to shed some light on an argument.

As a historical study, it will concern itself with events and change rather than in the accumulated past of the Church, but in the impact that history has made upon the Church and the Church upon history.

However, the relationship between history and the Church has a theological dimension. As McBrien argues:

> It has to do with the presence of grace in the world, with the direction and destiny of the world toward the kingdom of God, and with the role of the Church in proclaiming, celebrating, exemplifying, and saving the reality of grace.

This study grapples with three basic perspectives directly related to the Church's self-understanding (ecclesiology), the Church as an institution, community and servant.

The first was the dominant perspective in the pre-Vatican II period ... ; the second was encouraged by the (Second Vatican) Council itself . . . and the third was impelled by the activist concerns of the 1960's and a renewed appreciation of the Church's social doctrine.

Directly related to the three perspectives is the question of 'power'. As the Roman Catholic Church in Zimbabwe embarked on the process of implementing the Second Vatican Council's teachings, the transfer of 'power" from expatriate missionaries to a 'local church' became inherent. In an ecclesial setting, however, 'power' cannot have the same connotation as in a purely political context. Of course the Church is human; but it is at the same time divine. In spite of its human character, there remains a difference in her basic understanding of 'power' from a political (party) point of view.

## Plan of presentation

Part I consists of four chapters and explores developments from the midsixties up to the mid-seventies when the hierarchy started to update the Church's pastoral structures, from an institution-based to community-based model, in response to the teachings of Vatican II. Due account will be given to the response of the Catholic African Association and the Catholic lay teachers.

Part II, which also consists of four chapters, focuses on the Church as servant. It investigates the extent to which the Catholic Commission for Justice and Peace became an agent for change in the Church and society

INTRODUCTION                                                                 7

at large before and after independence. Here I also examine the extent to which the Commission became amenable to the aspirations and support of the local Church constituencies. In assessing the Commission's overall role I consider both the internal dynamics of transformation within the Catholic Church in Zimbabwe, and the external factors which affected the Church as the country went through the dramatic transition from U.D.I. and white minority rule to a free and democratic Zimbabwe.

## Notes

1. Randolph, R H *Dawn in Zimbabwe*, p.120.
2. Linden, I *The Catholic Church and the Struggle for Zimbabwe*, (1979) and D J Maxwell, 'A Study of the Roman Catholic Church — From Rhodesia to Zimbabwe (1950-86)' University of Manchester, BA dissertation, 1986. [Unpublished].
3. McLaughlin, J *On the Frontline: Catholic Missions in Zimbabwe's War*, Harare, Baobab Books, 1996.
4. Elton, G R *The Practice of History*, p.27.
5. Linden, *op.cit.*, p. 215.
6. *Ibid.*, pp. IX, XIII.
7. McLaughlin, J 'The Catholic Church and Zimbabwe's war of liberation: 1972-80'. D Phil thesis, UZ, 1991. p. 641.
8. Ranger, T O 'Holy men and rural communities in Zimbabwe: 1970-1980', in W J Sheils (ed.), *The Church and War*, Oxford, Blackwell, 1983, pp. 443-461.
9. Bourdillon, M F C and Gundani, P H 'Rural Christians and the Zimbabwe Liberation war', in C F Hallencreutz and A M Moyo (eds), *Church and State in Zimbabwe*, Gweru, Mambo Press, 1988, pp. 147-161.
10. Lan, D *Guns and Rain: Guerrillas and Spirit Mediums in Zimbabwe*, London, James Currey, 1985.
11. Auret, D *Reaching for Justice*, p. 177.
12. 'Power' is understood as 'the ability/capacity of one or more persons to realise their own will . . . against the will of others who are participating in the same act' cf. Galbraith J K, *The Anatomy of Power*, p.2.
13. McBrien, R P *Catholicism*, Minneapolis, Winston Press, 1981, p.605.
14. *Ibid.*, p.726.
15. Verstraelen, F F *An African Church in Transition: From Missionary Dependence to Mutuality in Mission*, Leiden, Inter-university Institute for Missiological and Ecumenical Research, 1975 pp. 4-15.

# PART I

## TOWARDS THE ERA OF THE 'LOCAL CHURCH'

## Chapter 1

# A New Emphasis in Ecclesiology

## Introduction

The Second Vatican Council's stress on the concept of the 'local church' came out of the need to rediscover the ecclesiological models of the early Christian Church. Over the centuries, since Constantine, in the fourth century, the Roman Catholic Church adopted an institutional model that became hierarchical, clerical and very Roman. After the Council of Trent in the 16th century, and particularly as the Church went through the era of Enlightenment, the institutional model grew stronger.

In Vatican II's documents, among others, the Dogmatic Constitution on the Church, *Lumen Gentium*, the 'local Church' is referred to as the locus 'in which the one, Holy, Catholic and Apostolic Church of Christ is truly present and operative'.[1] The Council documents teach that it is within the local congregation, that the faithful are gathered together by the preaching of the Gospel of Christ and the mystery of the Lord's Supper. Vatican II goes further to teach that in any community existing around an altar, under the sacred ministry of the bishop, there is manifested the symbol of that charity and unity of the mystical body, without which there can be no salvation.[2]

It would be a fallacy, however, to think that the post-conciliar communitarian ecclesiology removes the hierarchical character of the Church altogether. The latter dimension remains strong although modified through the collegial and co-responsible action of clergy and *episcopoi*. Bishops, priests, and deacons are singled out as those who exercise the ministerial priestly function in collaboration with the 'Vicar of Christ', the Pope.[3] In this sense, the structure or order is said to be constitutive, in the respect that the Church is never without some order, and cannot be described in merely functional terms.[4] Vatican II therefore views the hierarchical structure as necessary in helping the 'People of God' to fulfil the Church's mission in history.[5] Thus the parish is the focal point for carrying out this mission.

## The role of the parish in the development of the local church

A little history of the meaning of the word 'parish' may shed light on the development that the Roman Catholic Church has undergone over the centuries. In its Greek etymology 'parish', that is, *paroikia* denoted a district.

In Latin the corresponding term was *parochia*. As used in the early church, 'parish' meant an ecclesiastical area under the bishop and corresponded to what today is referred to as 'diocese'. From the fourth century it came to be applied to the subdivisions of the diocese which the bishop put in charge of resident presbyters (curate).[6] Up to the Second Vatican Council, 'parish' was considered to be such an administrative subdivision within the church. Such a concept led to the situation of crisis that the parish went through in the 1950's when more and more emphasis was put on the Church as 'the eucharistic fellowship'.[7] This concept became more articulated at the Second Vatican Council.

Due to the growth and flourishing theology of lay involvement championed by priests and theologians such as Y Congar, J Cardijn and others, there developed a crisis of expectation as the parish priest continued to operate as a factotum leader of the parish. Until then the 'power to rule and judge the people'[8] living in the parish and the power to administer to the parishioners the sacraments and other sacred duties were at the sole disposal of the parish priest. This monopoly of power was deemed incongruous in a Church that now gave the laity a place at the centre and not at the margins of its affairs at the local level as well as further up in the acclesiastical structures. A new concept of the parish had of necessity to be developed as the Catholic Church braced for the renewal that Pope John XXIII's *aggiornamento* called for.

According to the Second Vatican Council the parish is 'the living cell of the diocese, because it is the community organised locally under the guidance of a pastor representing a bishop'[9]. The parish is recognised as the most obvious expression of the corporate apostolate. Within it there is a wide variety of people gathered together in one assembly and united with the Church universal.

## Vatican II's emphasis on community fellowship

Vatican II, indeed, emphasised that the local Christian Community underlies the call to all Christians to be signs to others through mutual love and concern. In this spirit of fostering the development of the local church, Vatican II called for close cooperation between priests, the religious and the laity in each parish.

The priest, as a prudent cooperator with the bishop as well as its aid and instrument is called to serve the People of God in the local church. As a pastoral assistant of the Bishop he represents him in the individual parish. In a spirit of trust the priest is called is to teach, sanctify and govern under the bishop's authority.[10]

Furthermore, Vatican II teaches that the priest as pastor is not intended by Christ to shoulder the whole mission on his own. On the contrary, his

# Chapter 1 — A New Emphasis in Ecclesiology

task is one of co-ordination of the charisms and ministries which exist within a given local church, in order to see to it that 'all according to their proper roles may cooperate in this common undertaking with one heart (as a family)'[11].

The laity's cooperation with the priest is so much needed because without it the apostolate of the parish would be largely ineffectual. Lay people are expected to share actively in the liturgical life of their local community:

> to take part in its apostolic efforts ... attract back to the church those who have fallen away ... cooperate earnestly in preserving the teaching of God, particularly by catechetical instruction; by offering their own competencies they lend added efficiency to the care of souls and even to the management of church properties.[12]

The Vatican II also teaches that it is within the local church that lay members can bring to their assembly of the Church their own problems and questions of the world pertaining to salvation, for common debate, study, and resolution. They then can lend their energetic assistance to every apostolic and missionary programme of this, their ecclesial family.[13] In the Vatican II's most important document, 'On the Church', the lay apostolate is referred to as, 'a participation in the saving mission of the Church itself. Through their baptism and confirmation, all are commissioned to that apostolate by the Lord himself.[14]

Religious members attached to the local Church, that is the parish, can also contribute to the ecclesial family by being a sign of perfection through living in common and encouraging different forms of community assistance among various social groups and on behalf of those joined by common interests, such as, young people, women, workers, the sick, the unemployed etc.[15]

From the foregoing it is clear that Vatican II was, at least in theory, committed to a communitarian ecclesiology in which the energies of the participating members are fully tapped for the benefit of all and for the up building of the Church. The call for cooperation and co-responsibility among the laity, clergy and religious infuse a new understanding that the Church is at once lay, clerical and religious. Such an ecclesiology was not only radical but constituted a significant motivation towards pastoral renewal that Vatican II called for.

## Pastoral councils and the new ecclesiology

One of the aspirations of Vatican II was to update and adopt ecclesial operations and practices to the new attainments of the modern society. The spirit of the documents cited above reveal the desire to update the life of the church towards a participatory model. As the Western society was moving towards a general acceptance of democracy the Church had to adopt some democratic principles if it was not going to be viewed as an archaic institution in a fast-changing world.

As a practical step towards effecting the cooperation and co-responsibility of the clergy, laity and religious in the Church, Vatican II called for the establishment of pastoral councils. Such councils were to comprise the pastor, religious and lay members of the parishes in the diocese. In his pastoral letter, 'Ecclesia Sanctae', Pope Paul VI in 1967 recommended Church ordinaries to set up pastoral councils to facilitate regular meetings of the clergy, religious and lay people.[16] In this document the mandate of diocesan pastoral councils was 'to investigate and to weigh matters which bear on pastoral activity, and to formulate practical conclusions regarding them'[17]. The pastoral councils were designed to contribute not only in the affairs concerning finances, but also in opinion — making and in encouraging talents that could help in the administration of the diocese.

The Vatican Council, thus saw the Church as a network of dioceses that comprise parishes, each with a pastor and, if necessary, associate pastors. Within the setting of the parish the pastor was viewed as the living sign of the unity of those who are part of the local church and was expected to do his best to represent Christ by his service to all who came to him. However, before the Second Vatican Council, the pastor did virtually all of the administrative and pastoral work of the parish. This was the case particularly in a missionary environment such as in Rhodesia in the mid-1960s.

Vatican II, however, recommended regular meetings of the clergy, religious and lay people of the parish. It also encouraged inter-parochial meetings.[18] The Council went further to recommend that much of the administrative and pastoral work be taken over by competent lay people and lay boards.

The role of the Parish Council was to offer assistance in fostering pastoral action. As such it had a consultative role, while operating within the regulated norms established by the bishop.[19] While the pastor, associate pastors, and religious are ex-officio members of the parish council, lay members are elected to the council. Leaders of groups or associations that promote apostolic life of the parish are by virtue of their office co-opted to the council.

## Towards self-support

In keeping with the spirit of the Second Vatican Council, the 1983 code of canon law introduced a new provision for each parish to have a financial committee to help the pastors in the administration of the property of the parish. The members of the committee, who are selected according to the universal law and the norms of the diocese, assist the pastor of the parish without prejudice to canon 532 which states that the pastor represents the parish in all juridic affairs.[20]

According to Fr Michael McAuley, former lecturer in Canon Law at Chishawasha Regional Seminary in Zimbabwe, the code 'sees the finance

CHAPTER 1 — A New Emphasis in Ecclesiology                                15

committee as something separate from the parish council with its own membership'²¹. He goes on, however, to say that this committee is usually a part of the parish council made up of suitably qualified and experienced parish councillors with the treasurer as chairperson.²²

The ideas captured above constitue some of the norms forming the basis on which each 'particular' and 'local church' would, in its own way, try to implement the teachings of the Second Vatican. What follows below is an attempt to capture the history of implementation of the Second Vatican Council's teachings and recommendations pertaining to the development of the local church in the specific context of Zimbabwe.

## Notes

1.  *Lumen Gentium*, No. 26.
2.  *Ibid.*
3.  *Ibid.*, Nos. 26–29.
4.  McBrien, R *Catholicism*, p. 591.
5.  *Lumen Gentium*, No. 28.
6.  Cross, F L *Oxford Dictionary of the Christian Church*, p. 1061.
7.  Dulles, A *Models of the Church*, p. 9.
9.  Liebard O M *Clergy and Laity*, p. 312.
10. *Lumen Gentium*, No. 28.
11. *Ibid.*, No.30.
12. Decree on the Laity, No. 10.
13. *Ibid.*
14. *Lumen Gentium*, No. 33.
15. Liebard, *op.cit.*, p.312.
16. Paul VI, 'Ecclesia Sanctae', 6 August 1966, in Flannery, *Vatican Council II (The Conciliar and Post Conciliar Documents)*, pp. 591–610.
17. *Ibid.*
18. Decree on the Laity, No. 26.
19. Huels, J M *The New Canon Law for the Laity*, p.37.
20. *Ibid.*
21. McAuley, M 'Canon Law', *ZCBC Crossroads*, No. 119, 1988, p.13.
22. *Ibid.*
23. F J Verstraelem distinguishes 'particular church' from 'local church' by saying that the former refers to diocese while the latter 'can refer to a basic group like a parish' to the Church on a national level (in one cultural area) or a diocese in as far as it forms one more or less cohesive socio-cultural entity'. F J Verstraelen, *op.cit.*, p. 8. In this study 'local Church' refers to parish.

# Chapter 2

# Translating Vatican II into Practice in Zimbabwe

## Introduction

Since the call for the establishment of pastoral councils was made by the Pope in 1967 the implications of such a call were that the bishop/ordinary would have to appoint members of the clergy, religious, and laity who would assist him in the prioritisation of pastoral programmes. The bishop would naturally use his discretion in making such appointments. The result, therefore, was that the consultors were not formal representatives of the parishes and apostolic associations and groups. The fact that these appointees had not been elected by parishes and groups created problems of accountability, especially when the appointees claimed to speak on behalf of the groups or associations of which they were members.[1]

The alternative was to have parish council effectively function before proper pastoral councils were set up. Inevitably, those pastoral councils that were set up at the ordinary's discretion were a continuation of the monarchical model characteristic of the pre-Second Vatican Council era. To say this, however, is not to negate the possibility that they could have been effective. In some ways, however, these councils provided the transitional step towards the democratic ferment that later became part and parcel of parish communities.[2]

## The parish council

In late 1969 and early 1970 some effort was made by the Rhodesia Catholic Bishops' Conference (RCBC) to establish properly functioning parish council. Between 1967 and 1969 individual parishes had started with parish committees or mission committees, which were consultative bodies comprising members appointed by the pastor. All this was piecemeal to the extent that one could not say that a particular pattern was being evolved. While the majority of pastors lacked certainty of direction as a result of the Second Vatican Council's shift in ecclesiology, a few who were open to the new ideas, made helpful suggestions to the RCBC Secretariat which was set up by Rhodesia Catholic Bishops in 1967 to service all dioceses in the whole country. Since the mandate of the RCBC Secretariat was to collect and disseminate information pertaining to pastoral work, it naturally became the resource centre for bishops, dioceses and parishes. For instance, the few parishes that started to experiment with parish council had to send suggestions to the Secretariat about possible constitutions that would be adopted by the whole diocese.[4]

The efforts by few priests and parishes that got involved in the formation of parish council early were supported by the bishops who now viewed the need for the establishment of the local christian communities as an immediate priority. For instance, at an ordinary plenary session held at Umtali from 8 to 13 February 1971, the commission on catechetics noted the reduction of the subsidy from the Propaganda Fide and that it was becoming more and more difficult to subsidise pastoral projects.

Consequently, the Commission on Catechetics recommended the importance and necessity for catechists to be supported by their local church communities. To this end, the Commission noted, it was essential to have parish council widely established as a move towards self-sufficiency.

Apparently, the financial pressure from Rome was designed to be a catalyst for the change in ecclesiology streamlined by the Second Vatican Council. It had an impact on the pastoral endeavours of the clergy and religious in the field. Implied in such pressure was the fact that many clergy and religious were resistant to the change that the Vatican Council called for.

This resistance to the new order was pervasive in the Catholic Church in Rhodesia. Many priests were strongly opposed to the setting up of parish or pastoral councils. Both missionary and indigenous clergy were not ready to share responsibility with the laity. These clergy and religious, mostly trained before the Second Vatican Council, had become part and parcel of the untrammelled power that was associated with the mission-centreed Church. Those who had long-standing experience as parish priests before Vatican II had been at the helm of the administrative and judicial machinery of the parish. Most priests had enjoyed this power and its trappings and were not ready to let go.

Ironically, many indigenous seminarians of the late sixties were already talking about the need for the Third Vatican Council.[6] Having been products of missionary training and education, and having become part of the educated elite in a country that was marginally literate, many indigenous priests also regarded the participatory approach called by the Second Vatican Council as too early for the majority of Africans in the Church.[7]

It would be simplistic, however, to suggest that opposition emanated from the camp of clergy alone. It will be shown later, that opposition also emerged from the camp of the laity. In spite of the opposition from both the clergy and the laity, there are a number of factors, internal as well as external that led to the formation of parish council.

## The Sacred Congregation for the Evangelisation of Peoples

Developments in Zimbabwe were followed with interest from Rome. In July 1971 the Sacred Congregation for the Evangelisation of Peoples sent a questionnaire to the RCBC asking for a review of the church situation from 1950 up to 1970. The questionnaire provided an occasion for bishops in Rhodesia to launch a pastoral survey that was to make them aware of some of the problems and aspirations of their flock. Although the survey mainly concerned itself with reviewing previous pastoral programmes, it also left room for some focus on future priorities. From it, the bishops came up with recommendations that favoured the formation of local christian communities. The main accent of these recommendations was that the future of the church in Zimbabwe lay in Africanisation. This in effect implied that there was need for the Church to become that of the local people.[8]

The process of forming local communities involved, *inter alia*, the handing over of responsibilities to Africans in all sectors, in specific terms making greater efforts to relinquish responsibility to the laity and to increase lay training as a method of empowerment.[9]

## The Lavoie survey

The findings from the survey carried out for Propaganda Fide sparked some interest and curiosity among the bishops of Rhodesia. In an unexpected move, the RCBC called for another survey to be launched. The aim of the survey was to measure the functional effectiveness of church structures from the standpoint of those involved pastorally and its goal was to provide information which would be used as a basis for taking concrete steps towards improving them. For this survey the RCBC enlisted the services of a Canadian pastoral anthropologist and theologian, Fr W F Lavoie.

The survey by Fr Lavoie, which was carried out between August and October 1972 was addressed to pastors and religious who were involved in parish work. However, the catechists who were also engaged in parish work were left out and so were the laity, including the many teachers who were leading in the pastoral activities of the mission outstations. At most, the hierarchy sent 1 500 questionnaires to lay people, not to consult them as such, but for the sole purpose of informing them that the survey was being carried out.[10]

Fr Lavoie's findings confirmed earlier insights by the bishops. The desire to build realistic and strong Christian communities and the recognition of the need for pastoral planning toward this end were repeatedly evident.

Some respondents to Fr Lavoie's survey felt that a good start towards establishing the local church was already under way through the introduction of parish council. According to Fr Lavoie's findings a substantial number of priests viewed parish council as positive and effective.[12] Stepping up the establishment of Parish council was therefore viewed as constituting the first practical steps towards the establishment of a strong local church and the implementation of the teachings of the Second Vatican Council.

The survey clearly showed signs of a Church in transition, living in the past but struggling towards the future. Among the major weaknesses of the report was the failure to enlist the thinking and opinion of the laity. The most that the hierarchy did was a symbolic action of sending 1 500 questionnaires to some lay persons. Nobody knows what symbolic results this action was meant to achieve. However, as already noted above, the questionnaires sent out were not meant to consult or to elicit the opinion of the laity but merely to inform them that the survey was being carried out.[13]

Leaving out the laity in the fact-finding stages of planning and policy change clearly manifested entrenched clericalism that thrived on perceptions of power interests. As a healthy contrast we see the introduction, in 1968, of the Roman Catholic Council for the Laity.

## The National Catholic Council for the Laity

In 1968 the Roman Catholic National Council for the Laity in Rhodesia was formed. Its formation was in response to the call by the Second Vatican Council for territorial and international lay councils to be formed. The highest administrative body for such councils was the lay Secretariat in Rome.

The Roman Catholic National Council for the Laity in Rhodesia served as an interdiocesan body with a mandate to coordinate lay activities in the whole country. Although little is known about its constitution and how it became defunct in the late seventies, what is pertinent at this stage is that in its first two years of existence it composed the first constitutional *typicum* for the parish council. The typicum received the approval by the RCBC *ad experimentum* for three years.[14] Worked out in the spirit of the Second Vatican Council, the *typicum* was supposed to be sent to missions and parishes as the guiding principle (canon) in the establishment of parish council as the first step towards building up the local church.

By the end of 1970 the Archbishop of Salisbury sent out the constitutional *typicum* to all parishes under him. Accompanying the *typicum* was a covering letter, in which Archbishop Francis Markall requested all his parish clergy and existing parish mission committees to carefully consider the *typicum* as the basis for the updating of the parish constitutions that had been in use before.[15]

The Archbishop of Salisbury readily accepted the typicum from the National Council of the Laity. The alacrity in dispatching the typicum to parishes in his diocese was evident of his desire to see parish council established as soon as possible. However, this does not mean that the idea to set up parish council was implemented faster and earlier in the Archdiocese of Salisbury than in others.

Up to the end of 1971 the Roman Catholic National Council for the Laity was mainly oriented towards two goals: the formation of active christian communities and the teaching of the faith by parents and volunteers to children. The latter goal emerged from the handover of primary schools to local councils by the church which was a result of the changes in the Government's education policy in 1969/70, and which we will discuss in detail in the next chapter.[16] More energy, however, was exerted towards the establishment of local parish council or church committees in which the laity shared responsibility for the building up of a strong and active local church.[17]

A progress report from the meeting of the Roman Catholic National Council for the Laity held in February 1971 indicated that the formation of parish council was under way in some dioceses. The Salisbury Archdiocese topped the list with thirteen parish councils whilst the Umtali Diocese had only one, at Chipinge. In both dioceses there were incipient diocesan councils that were involved in setting up Parish council since 1971. The Archdiocese of Salisbury was the first to have a diocesan pastoral council composed of clergy, laity and the bishop. This council then appointed people who would spearhead the formation of parish council.[18]

In the Diocese of Gwelo a meeting was held at Gokomere Mission in early 1971 to consult lay bodies about the formation of parish council. From this meeting it was hoped that a diocesan council for the laity would be formed before the end of 1971, and that such a council would be charged with the responsibility for encouraging the formation of parish council. In the diocese of Wankie, a congress of the laity was held at Kana mission in August 1971, apparently to encourage the formation of parish council.[20]

In an annual report for 1972 the National Council for the Laity reported that diosesan councils of the lay apostolate had now been established in Bulawayo, Gwelo and Umtali. Salisbury had a pastoral council, not a lay council. The Roman Catholic Council of the Laity, however, viewed the Salisbury council with cynicism. It was referred to in their reports as 'the Diocesan pastoral council (so called in Salisbury).'[21] Though constitutionally different, in as far as the formation of parish council, the Salisbury diocesan pastoral council was the equivalent of the diosesan council for the laity. The National Council for the Laity annual report for 1972 states that the diocesan

CHAPTER 2 — Towards the Era of the 'Local Church'  21

councils of the laity were putting every possible effort into the establishment of parish council in all areas. It goes on to say that more and more responsibility for the work of the Church was being handled by the parish council wherever they were formed.[22]

As noted earlier on, the process of change was much more complex than the history of the efforts of one organisation like the National Catholic Council for the Laity. Such a history would not be complete without highlighting the opposing forces or agents of restraint operating from within the Church.

## The Catholic Association and the innovations of the Second Vatican Council

As stated above, the National Council for the Laity came about as a result of the Second Vatican Council. It started to operate at the national level as an interdiocesan coordinating body.[23] At its formation in 1968, the National Council came into conflict with the Catholic Association, a lay organisation that claimed to be the chief coordinator of all Catholic lay undertakings in Rhodesia.[24] Since the Association will come up for discussion later on in this study, it is necessary to say more about what it was and what it represented in the Roman Catholic Church in Rhodesia.

The Catholic Association (CA) was formed in Southern Rhodesia in 1953, and was then known as the Catholic African Association (CAA).[25] The idea of forming the Association came from the Catholic African Union which had been started by Fr Bernard Huss of Mariannhill in Natal in 1934.[26] The aim of the CA in southern Rhodesia was to unite all Catholics irrespective of their profession. Article 2 (a) of its 1953 constitution states its aim as to promote unity in Catholic Action under the guidance of ecclesiastical authority.'[27]

Later in 1966, after the Second Vatican Council, the Association modified its aim to read 'to help its members to bring Christ to their world by being His witness and His living instrument.'[28]

Of interest in the change of the Association's aim is the fact that the former stressed the dominance of the clergy while the latter stressed the role of the laity and their own understanding of Catholic faith. This change of perspective in the Association's aim will become clearer later when we discuss the process of transformation that occurred from 1968 to 1973.

It was the CAA that founded a Catholic magazine that was earlier on called by its name, *The Catholic African Association* (the magazine was launched at the CAA congress held at Gokomere Mission from 21 to 23 August, 1959). In January 1960 the magazine's name was changed to *Moto*.[29]

Well before 1959, members of the CAA had stressed the need for a Catholic magazine or newspaper which would provide Catholics with 'a reliable source of information'. This call came about because of the campaign of misinformation emanating from the government media. Thus at its founding the CAA/Moto magazine aimed at providing 'a reliable source of information' on religious and Church issues with direct bearing on the Catholic Church.[30] After the Second Vatican Council, however, Moto was given some reorientation; 'it became no longer strictly a Catholic paper nor was it limited only to Church news'.[31]

The Association flourished up to the early seventies because of the support it got from some of its dedicated spiritual advisors, especially the following members of the Society of Jesus, Fr Michael Hannan, Fr Francis Markall (later Archbishop of Salisbury), and Fr John Dove. In the diocese of Gwelo Fr Joseph Elsener stood out in support of the Association.[32]

The Catholic African Association later changed its name to the Catholic Association (CA), to express its non-racial character and was registered in August, 1971 as a welfare organisation under the Welfare Organisations Act (1966). In spite of its assumed non-racial character since 1971, a few whites from Marandellas who became members of the Association in 1971 lasted three months. That was the first and only time for the Association to have non-black members.[33]

At the time that the National Catholic for Council of the Laity was formed the hierarchy argued that there was need for an all-embracing lay organisation that would represent lay interestes. In the hierarchy's opinion the CAA, which was a fee — paying organisation, could not represent the interests of all Catholics. By 1968 there were many pious associations such as Sodalities, Legion of Mary and others, which were playing a prominent role outside the confines of the CAA. Furthermore there were many lay Catholics who did not identify with any apostolic association and therefore would not have their interests represented in the CAA.[34]

The CAA had representative structures at parish, regional, diocesan and national levels.[35] By virtue of these structures the CAA became a bastion of resistance to the changes that the hierarchy wanted to introduce in the Church. Meanwhile, the CAA was viewed by many black Catholics as a successful experiment towards adopting a lay Catholic organisation to the African context. It was viewed as an organisation with huge potential of adapting lay African spirituality to the African context. This is why its congresses were regarded as most interesting and, more often than not, were well attended.[36]

The formation of the Roman Catholic Council for the Laity in 1968 and the Diosesan Councils for the Laity in the early seventies implied that the role and function claimed by the Catholic African Association was superseded, not only at national and diocesan levels, but also at the parish level, because the former organizations called for the formation of all-embracing parish council.[37] The anticipated change did not come easy, however. Many members of the CAA and some priests were not prepared to defer to the Roman Catholic Council for the Laity, supported by the hierarchy, without first putting up a bold fight. The ensuing conflict demands a region to region analysis in order to avoid generalisations.

## Regional survey

### Gwelo diocese

Gwelo diocese was not among the dioceses which early on set up the Diocesan Council for the Laity or parish council. The reason was that neither organization could exist side by side with the CAA. At a regional congress at Holy Cross Mission in September, 1969, Mr Raphael Paradza made reference to the growing conflict between CAA and the members who wanted to see the formation of a parish council. The CAA's resistance to change was described as worrying.

The conflict between the CAA and the movement towards parish council raged on for years. It was made worse by the fact that many priests and laity did not understand the terms of reference of the National Council for the Laity and at local level its relation to the CAA.[40] Because of this growing concern, discussions and negotiations were entered into between the CAA and the diocesan authorities culminating in the formation of the Diocesan Council of the Lay Apostolate (DCLA) at a meeting of mission and parish representatives held at Gokomere Mission from 7 to 9 December, 1972.[41] The conflict had therefore raged on for three years. After this historic meeting the Gwelo CAA was dissolved and was replaced by the DCLA with Fr Xavier Marimazhira in charge as coordinator of the training of laity at Gokomere Centre for the laity.

After this consensual dissolution of the Gwelo chapter of the CAA, it was now possible to form parish council. At an ordinary plenary session of the bishops in 1973, Bishop Haene reported that many parish council were set up. The bishop attributed the successes in his diocese to the enthusiasm of African Catholics who had come forward to take on responsibility.[42]

### Archdiocese of Salisbury

In the Salisbury archdiocese the CAA was not viewed as a source of problems in the same way that it was in Gwelo. The experience here was that the Association was accepted as one of the member associations represented in the parish council and the pastoral council. As opposed to dioceses like Gwelo where the CAA grew to be the sole powerful partner alongside the hierarchy, in Salisbury it was one of the many lay groups and associations. In the latter diocese the CAA could not claim sole lay representation at parish or diocese level. Because of this plurality the CAA was not asked to dissolve its membership at the time that parish council were formed.

It would be inaccurate, however, to argue that no friction existed between the hierarchy, priests and the laity in the archdiocese of Salisbury. A survey carried out in 1969 by Mr Ralph Tanner for the archdiocese showed that in some parishes the proper function of the Parish Council was achieved not without some clash with the clergy. At St Agnes parish in New Highfield, there was a level of lay enthusiasm which was viewed as disadvantageous to the proper function of the Parish Council.[43] Although there is no specific reference to the CAA as the source of disturbances at St Agnes, interviews with lay members indicate that the parish was once a stronghold of the CAA in the sixties and seventies.[44] The instance of St Agnes parish, perhaps shows that there may have been isolated cases of clashes between the CAA and the new movement towards the formation of parish council. The clashes, however, did not deteriorate to the crisis levels that were seen in Gwelo.

### Umtali diocese

The situation in Umtali diocese differed from that in Gwelo and Salisbury. In Umtali no attempts to dissolve the CAA were made, nor were attempts made to co-opt members or leaders of the CAA into the parish council structure. A totally new approach was adopted. The CAA boards and councils were upgraded into parish council. This was followed by a reorientation of the councils to meet the requirements of the new lay responsibilities.

### Bulawayo and Wankie dioceses

The CAA had not yet been established in the dioceses of Wankie and Bulawayo. Bulawayo had a different type of lay movement, which was the Catholic African Union (CAU) derived from Marrianhill in South Africa. Members of the union did not join the CAA[46] Wankie did not have either the CAA or the CAU. In the case of Bulawayo, however, it is not at all clear whether there were problems or not when parish council were being formed. However, it is worth mentioning that both dioceses convened lay congresses before the end of 1972, with the aim of reorienting the laity towards the new ecclesiological structures based on parish and diocesan councils.[47]

### Conclusion

The crisis of opinion that affected the Catholic Church in Rhodesia during the late sixties and early seventies can be viewed as inevitable pangs that accompanied the birth of a new ecclesiology that pushed for a shift from hierarchical domination to lay — clergy co-responsibility. The change which the Second Vatican Council, and subsequently the Rhodesian hierarchy wanted to see, however positive it may have been, was not readily embraced by its would — be beneficiaries because it came from the top. It was not based on a thorough education and consultation of the laity. Without this it was inevitable that such change would be met with resistance. Clearly, the Roman Catholic Church in Rhodesia of the sixties and early seventies was still far from being people-based and participatory in approach. The clergy, not least the bishops, were yet to learn to share responsibilities with the laity, who together with all believers constituted the christifidelis.

## Notes

1. Memo from General Secretary to Archbishop, October, 1970, p.1. Box on Parish council, Jesuit Archives
2. Ibid., p.3.
3. Ibid., p.4.
4. Ibid., p.5.
5. RCBC Newsletter, No.8, March, 1971 p.7.
6. Niederberger O., *The African clergy in the Catholic Church in Rhodesia*, p.12.
7. Ibid.
8. RCBC File 21/19. Cf. RCBC Plenary Session; Umtali. Re. Questionnaire from Rome, No. 3787/21, June, 1970, p.17.
9. Ibid.
10. RCBC Newsletter, No. 29, December, 1972, p. 10
11. Ibid.
12. Ibid.
13. Supra, pp. 28-29.
14. Memo from RCBC General Secretary to Bishop Haene (President of RCBC) May, 1969. (RCBC Archives)
15. Memo on Parishes from Bishop Markall, August, 1971. (Harare archdiocese Archives)
16. Randolph R H, *Church and State in Rhodesia*, p.22.
17. RCBC Newsletter, No. 21, April, 1972, p.10.
18. Ibid.
19. RCBC Newsletter, No. 10, May, 1971, p.3.

20. Ibid.
21. *Ibid.*
22. RCBC Newsletter, No. 30, January, 1973, p.19.
23. Supra, p.30.
24. Jesuit Archives Box 319 & 393/5, the Catholic Association
25. cf. Jesuit Archives, File entitled, 'Brief History of the Catholic Association (C.A)' Registration No. W.O. 32/71, p.1.
26. *Ibid.*
27. *Ibid.*
28. *Ibid.*
29. *Ibid.*, p. 2
30. *Ibid.*, p. 9.
31. *Ibid.*
32. *Ibid.*
33. *Ibid.*, p.2.
34. *Ibid.*, This was Bishop Haene's argument at a CA Meeting in Gwelo, May, 1971.
35. *Ibid.*
36. Jesuit Archives, Box 319/5.
37. RCBC Newsletter, No. 21, April, 1972, p.10.
38. Supra, p.32.
39. Jesuit Archives, Box 393/5 (Cf. Parish councils).
40. RCBC Newsletter, No. 30, January 1973, p.5.
41. Jesuit Archives, Box 393/5.
42. RCBC Newsletter, No. 30, January, 1973, p.5.
43. R Tanner's Report, September, 1969. (Jesuit Archives, Box 153/2)
44. Interviews at St. Agnes, Highfield with Parish Council Executives, 29 August 1992.
45. Jesuit Archives, Box 393/5 (Cf. Parish council).
46. *Ibid.*
47. RCBC Newsletter, No.30, January, 1973, p.5.

Chapter 3

# Church Renewal and Challenges from the Minority Regime: the Problem over the Church Schools

## Introduction

In the previous chapter we outlined the activities and pace of the Church in establishing the parish, diocesan and pastoral councils. These structures were the first steps adopted in fostering a new post-conciliar ethos of co-responsibility between the clergy and laity. Important as these steps were, they were simply preliminary overtures in a complex process of transformation that affected the church as it moved into the 1970s.

In this chapter the focus will be on the church-run schools which up to 1971 had provided the main locus for evangelisation. However, because of the new education policy announced by the Smith regime in September 1969, the Church was forced to surrender its authority over primary schools.[1]

In order to appreciate the importance that was attached to church-run primary schools in respect of evangelisation, we will first outline their function and the methods used in order to meet their intended goals. Secondly, we will illustrate the church-state conflict that ensued subsequent to the passing of the New Education Bill of 1969. Finally, we will assess the immediate impact that the loss of church-run schools had on missionary strategies regarding evangelisation and indeed on the movement towards the ideal of the 'local church'.

## The Church-run school system

Up until 1970 the Roman Catholic Church's missionary methods were to a large extent concentrated on the Church schools. These schools were owned and administered by members of missionary orders based at central mission stations.[2] The central primary schools had, since the 1940's become centres of christian formation. According to Randolph, once Secretary General of the Rhodesia Catholic Bishops Conference, the church had not involved itself in education for the sole reason of teaching academic or industrial skills, 'but to teach the Catholic faith and morals.'[3] The primary schools as significant means of evangelisation became the rationale for the Church to contribute financially towards their running. Together with local parents in the rural areas the Church contributed 'all the capital finance for the schools at no cost to the government'.[4] However, the government paid salary grants for the teachers.

From the end of the Second World War in 1945, the Church expanded its operations in the educational field. This expansion was attributed to the consistent influx of missionary personnel into Rhodesia. The Bethlehem Fathers gained a substantial increase in personnel and were given Apostolic Prefecture status over Fort Victoria region in 1947.[5] Five years later the Spanish Burgos Fathers and the Carmelite Fathers, who also joined the missionary field once dominated by the Jesuit order, and the Marriannhill Fathers in the mid-forties, were given independent Prefecture statuses over Wankie[6] and Umtali[7] areas, respectively. As noted above all these new missionary regions later gained diocesan status.

The coming of more missionary societies to Rhodesia led to the establishment of more Church-run primary schools in rural areas. This increase in schools brought about a corresponding increase in the numbers of baptised children. In 1950 when the church had few schools, baptised Catholics only constituted 3,7 per cent of the population. However, by 1970 when the Church boasted of 1 050 primary schools, the baptised Catholics now constituted 8,7 per cent of the population.[8]

The swelling of numbers of baptised Catholics has been rightly attributed to the Church-run primary schools. According to the *Rhodesia Catholic Bishops' Conference Newsletter* the practice in the schools was that 'many children were baptised before the end of the course . . . The largest number of catechumens came from among primary school pupils.'[9] This increase in catechumens occurred in rural areas where the Church of the 1950s and the 1960s extended her sole operations.[10]

A number of factors influenced the pupils, who enrolled at Catholic schools, to join the Church. Denominational competition among the missionaries caused some priests to adopt the policy of 'no religion no place in school'. This policy put pressure on pupils who enrolled in Catholic schools. Although this practice was not explicitly stated in any mission policy of the Church, it became commonly practised in areas where there was much competition with Protestant churches.[11]

According to observations of one priest, pupils were not given much room to deliberate before becoming catechumens. The pupils, as expected, 'asked for and accepted baptism as part of their schooling and never realised they were voluntarily attaching themselves to Christ'.[12]

CHAPTER 3 — *Church Renewal and Challenges from the Minority Regime* 29

The influence that the Church school had on the young is captured in reminiscences of individuals that were interviewed. Pupils who went to Catholic school got used to catholic prayers and liturgy.[13] To the young boys, things like serving at the altar, an exercise that only Catholic boys performed, influenced some non-Catholics to register for Catechism. The desire to become altar-servers resulted in permanent membership within the Catholic church.[14] Peer pressure often played an important part in such decisions.[15]

Although non-Catholic parents would have wanted to send their children to schools of their own denominational affiliation such schools were sometimes too few and far between. As a result their children had to enrol at a Catholic school. On their own, the young children got attracted to the Church and converted.[16]

## The new education policy

In 1966, only a year after the conclusion of the Second Vatican, in 1966, the Rhodesian Government announced a new policy on education. The policy limited the involvement of churches in African education. This policy had multiple implications on the operations of the churches. Firstly, it sought to restrain churches from opening new salary grant-aided primary schools. Secondly, it prohibited the opening of additional streams in existing salary grant-aided schools. Thirdly, it prohibited the opening of any new grant-aided upper primary classes in Tribal Trust Lands and African Purchase Areas.[17]

The reaction from the Catholic Church to these new measures was rather weak and uncoordinated. Although the bishops expressed consternation at the fact that they were not consulted by the Government, they abided by the new policy. However, according to Fr R. Randolph, the bishops saw this move by the government as a bad omen for the future relations between Church and State.[18]

In September, 1969 the Minister of Education announced a new education policy that was to have serious consequences for the operations of the churches in education. The Minister made it known that as from 1971 Government would pay 'only 95 per cent of the salaries of teachers in African aided primary schools — not, let it be noticed, of teachers in African government schools'.[19] This notification was accompanied by the condition that if aided schools were to continue under the present responsible authorities, almost all of which were mission organisations, the authorities themselves would have to make good the five per cent deduction.[20] The responsible authorities were asked to make good the five per cent cut from their financial resources or by charging additional fees from their pupils and their parents. If they could not meet these requirements, then they were required to surrender their schools to other responsible authorities, that is, local African Councils under the Ministry of Local Government.[21]

The Rhodesia Front government argued that the five per cent cut was necessary in order for government to fund an expansion in secondary education for the Africans. The new education policy was viewed by the Catholic Church as an instrument deliberately designed to force the Church out of primary schools. The policy was also seen as a political ploy aimed at forcing local African communities to form councils in accordance with the Native Council Act of 1957.[22]

The Native Councils Act had elicited heavy opposition from the African National Council.[23] A few years earlier, in 1963, Winston Field had attempted to implement the Councils Act under the guise of community development programmes. This attempt had not succeeded due to popular opposition. The scheme was subsequently dropped.[24] The Catholic bishops had then joined forces with the African masses in opposing Winston Field's community development policies. They had warned that the policies 'could be used to promote or bring about separate development and permanent racial or tribal divisions.'[25]

The new education policy promulgated in 1969 was therefore viewed in political light as a resuscitation of the Rhodesia Front Community Development programme, and in line with the Land Apportionment Act (1931), that had divided Rhodesia racially. The latter was further entrenched by the 1969 Land Tenure Act. As the Anglican Bishop John Burrough aptly noted, the Rhodesia Front government was not serious about furthering African interests in education. Instead it was seen as experimenting with a Bantustan form of administration like that started in South Africa.[26]

Faced with the two options, either to make good the five per cent cut or hand over primary schools to local councils, the Catholic bishops consulted other Church authorities on what decision to make. These consultations finally led to the Heads of Denominations meeting which issued a public statement on 25 November 1969, refusing 'to be held responsible for a reduction (five per cent cut) made by a unilateral decision on the part of the government'.[27]

At the Heads of Denominations meeting on 25 November, the Church leaders, except the Anglican Bishop of Mashonaland, John Burrough and the Roman Catholic Bishop of Gwelo, A. Haene, decided to hand over the schools to local councils or to the Government. The position of the majority was based on the fact that they could not provide the considerable sum which would be required, and that they were 'not prepared to be tax collectors on behalf of the government'.[28] In his reflections on this Heads of Denominations meeting, Kenneth Skelton, the former Bishop of the Anglican diocese of Bulawayo, argued that even if the churches could have collected the money from donations or from parents of enrolled pupils (alternatives which Bishops Burrough and Haene of Gwelo were keen to explore), 'they would inevitably have shared the odium aroused by this imposition'.[29]

It was not going to be easy for the churches to accept levying fees on pupils in order to meet the 5 per cent cut in teachers' salaries. Such an alternative was found to be burdensome on African parents, who all along from the 1940s were paying 35 per cent of the school grant per child. The Catholic Church's estimates for 1970 alone were, that each one of the five dioceses would have to collect £15000 per year from African parents.[30]

The decision by the Heads of Denominations should of course be considered within the context of the political crisis gripping Rhodesia since the 1965 'Unilateral Declaration of Independence' (UDI) by I.D. Smith. It was important for the church leaders to be seen to be in sympathy with the suffering African majority. The refusal by the church leaders to levy more fees on pupils should therefore be viewed as symbolic of the churches' political allegiance to the African people. Considering also the low economic situation of Africans, the majority of whom were subsistence farmers with a gross agricultural output approximately one quarter of that of white farmers,[31] the decision to hand over schools was politically correct.

As noted above, one of the five Roman Catholic Bishops, A. Haene, of Gwelo, took a position different from that of the rest of his Catholic colleagues and the Heads of Denominations.[32] He wanted to hold on to the schools in his diocese, and had openly expressed this decision 'both in the Bishops' Conference and in the Heads of Denominations meetings.'[33] Bishop A. Haene was prepared to find ways of raising money to subsidise the primary schools and did not think that the Heads of Denominations and the Bishops' Conference were adopting the best solution by handing over schools to local councils. In his view, it was better to assist the 'already over-burdened African parents' financially and prepare them to take over the schools in due course.[34] This would be a better form of moral protest against the imposition by the Government. Furthermore, Bishop Haene, (and all Heads of Churches concurred), was concerned at the fact that the local Councils to whom the Churches were to hand over schools, 'simply did not exist'[35]. In areas where they existed, they were 'not up to the task of running a complex of primary schools'.[36] More than the other bishops, Haene was concerned that the majority of the African people, except a small elite, did not understand the issues at stake and that there was therefore the risk that government might be able to convince them that the churches were leaving them in the lurch.

At the insistence of Bishop Haene in continuing with the primary schools in his diocese, the Heads of Denominations accepted that he could take an independent course of action in his diocese. After a series of meetings with the rest of the Catholic bishops, Haene was influenced against standing out of line with the rest of the dioceses.[38] Although the desire for Haene's change of mind may be viewed as an attempt by the Catholic Church to maintain unity of action, such uniformity remained superficial. The thinking in the Gwelo diocese remained unchanged: the Church had not served the best interests of the people in this instance, since the decision of the dioceses was based on material grounds, and that these grounds were not particularly convincing.[39]

It is necessary to explain at this stage what Bishop Haene and his diocese viewed as leaving the Africans in the lurch. To relinquish schools meant that the Church would forthwith withdraw her financial support that she had traditionally given to the schools which she administered. Such withdrawal of funds meant leaving the financial burden on the shoulders of African parents. In the few places where local Councils existed, parents were to pay what the Council levied on each pupil. In areas where there were no Councils, schools were to be taken over and sponsored by central government for a minimum of two years and up to a maximum of five years. Parents were to pay a special fee of $1.25 per term per child in addition to the building fund which varied from school to school depending on the development under way. This was higher than the fees that were being paid by each child when the schools were under Church authority.[40]

In light of the economic status of most rural Africans, it was likely that the increased financial burden would lead to some children dropping out of these schools. According to Sr Gemma Chifamba (LCBL), female pupils were increasingly more affected by the drop-outs. Some parents started lapsing back to the outmoded tradition in which only boys would be prepared to be migrant workers while girls stayed at home waiting for marriage.[41]

In 1970 in the Archdiocese of Salisoury alone, 178 out of 1 272 girls failed to sit for their Grade 5 examinations and in 1971, a further drop of 546 out of 1 955 girls failed to sit for the examinatons.[42] Considering the adverse implications of the government's new education Bill on the rural African peoples, it is difficult to believe Linden's assertion that Many Africans in rural areas welcomed the possibility of removing schools from the church into the hands of the African Council.[43]

Ian Linden does not, however, substantiate this assertion. The problem with Linden's suggestion, that rural Africans shared little concern over who controlled schools, and that the rural Africans were ready 'to take on the running of primary education without preparation when called upon,' is its

CHAPTER 3 — *Church Renewal and Challenges from the Minority Regime*      33

implication, that African parents were so unpoliticised that they were ready to accept the Government's imposition without question. His view also suggests that the rural Africans were not aware of the financial implications of such change or that they had the financial wherewithal to meet the demands that the change from the Churches to Councils brought upon them. Such a position also implies that the rural Africans had forgotten about the 'popular resistance' that they had made to the community development policy of 1963. Furthermore, Linden fails to understand why the Heads of Denominations rejected the government's policy. Their rejection was a protest against the government's imposition rather than an acceptance of the councils' option.

The surrender of schools which was adopted by the majority of Catholic bishops and especially championed by Bishop Donal Lamont, was meant to be a political coup. In Bishop Lamont's view the Church's pulling out of the schools would result in the schools having to be closed, since the rural people were not prepared to take over. Such eventuality would 'make the situation clear-cut in terms of knowing who the Africans' real enemy was. As a result of the withdrawal the African people would defend the church even in times of persecution by the State.[45]

In the end, Bishop A. Haene opted for a gradual hand-over policy arguing that the sudden withdrawal would lead the Church to lose influence over the people.[46] His position was, however, more than simply moral; it was also utilitarian. It was a result of the lack of diversification, on the part of the missionary Church, in the field of evangelisation. Perhaps Haene's desire to maintain the schools could be viewed as a way of protecting the Church's institutional interests.[47] The majority position against community development was not really a defence for the churches and their schools but a response to the moral and political crisis that the nation faced. The decision should be seen in the light of the reinforced critique of the Land Tenure Act (1969), whose goals were to promote or bring about separate development and permanent racial and tribal divisions.[48]

The fact that all catholic bishops finally agreed to hand over their primary schools to the Government or to local Councils had far-reaching implications for future approaches to evangelisation. The surrender of schools in fact comprised a turning point in the history of ecclesiology in Zimbabwe. Up until 1971, the missionary church had depended on institutions such as schools, hospitals, orphanages and the like. This system had exposed the Church to the risk of being understood more in terms of power over, instead of service to, the people. In the continued discussion we will show how the school system had functioned up until 1971, and the ecclesiological impact that the surrender of schools had on the Church.

## The school as power base for the Church

As already stated above, the Catholic primary school was crucial in the formation of the Christian character of the young.[49] In 1968, the Catholic Church alone had 1 050 primary and secondary schools with a total of 88 795 baptised young Catholics.[50] It was for this reason that many religious orders had a substantial percentage of teacher-priests who were mainly preoccupied with the teaching apostolate.[51] The obvious advantage with this system was that the teacher-priests found a good opportunity to cultivate Christian values and character within the young boys and girls at a very tender age. Though secondary, another advantage was that teacher-priests were paid by the government, and their salaries maintained other priests who engaged in pastoral work.[52]

The disadvantage of this system, however, was that the school model unwittingly forced the Church to become increasingly dependent on the Government. Critics of the Church school model argued that such dependence on Government often led to a situation where African lay teachers had an insignificant role when involved in political policies of which the latter disapproved. The people who negotiated for them were their employers, the bishops.[53] The teacher-priests as well as mission superiors were the managers of the rural primary schools which fell under the authority of the diocesan bishops.

The involvement of the clergy at administrative and managerial levels also had negative implications on their overall pastoral performance. It resulted in their being overworked. Consequently they 'found little time or leisure for pastoral planning and review and less enthusiasm for attending (pastoral) meetings'.[54]

In such a system, the lay African teacher became 'the assistant pastoral worker of the priest... as well as the indispensable link between the missionary and the new Christians.'[55] Many lay teachers were obliged to teach the Church's doctrine and catechetical education to pupils enrolled in the school. They were expected to prepare the pupils for sacraments of baptism, confession, confirmation and the eucharist, as well as to lead Sunday services without the priest.[56]

These duties were not necessarily accepted by the lay teachers. One teacher, whose observations expressed the sentiments of many others, contends that most teachers forfeited their secular commitments in order to lead or attend to church services and to teach catechism. He went further to explain:

> Those who did not oblige were black-listed, and were often not promoted. Others were even fired. However, a sizeable number were loyal and devoted Catholics. These worked without complaining. The government of the Church gave us no option.

Hence most of us went on performing duties that we would not have voluntarily done had we been asked to choose. One had to do it liking or not.[57]

Some priests were aware of the compulsive mechanism inherent in the Church school system. According to Fr Paul Edwards (SJ), teachers were unable to say 'no' to the religious duties that the priests expected them to carry out. The problem was that the careers of lay teachers were dependent on the priest managers' impression of them as 'good Catholics'.[58] As a matter of survival:

> many a teacher saw the importance of 'chatting up Father', when he came to visit the school. It became a formality and therefore, not necessarily a sincere gesture.[59]

The power relationship that applied between priest and lay teachers also obtained between teacher and pupil. As E. Callaghan argued, the convenience of the priest and that of the school teacher were often given first consideration, while that of the catechumen was given second-rate consideration.[60]

In spite of the contradiction inherent in the school system, many missionaries took solace in the fact that through the school they catered for the population that mattered most in the future of the nation, that is those under fifteen.[61] According to Allen Best, approximately 48 per cent of the African population was, in 1970, under fifteen.[62]

At this stage it is appropriate also to refer to the findings of a pastoral anthropologist, Ralph Tanner, who carried out a survey in May, 1969 in the Jesuit dominated Archdiocese of Salisbury. His findings and recommendations applied to the situation that obtained in 1969 and 1970 in the Catholic Church in Rhodesia.

According to Tanner, most priests in the Salisbury Archdiocese wanted to continue to own and run schools.[63] In his recommendations to the Vicar General of the Archdiocese of Salisbury, Tanner argued that, If the care of the souls is the preoccupation of the Society then a practical withdrawal from this involvement should be considered.[64]

In his view the Church school system was biased against parents. He therefore called for a balance to be created in catering for the young and the old.[65]

Basing his observations on experiences of the Church in East Africa, Tanner argued that concentration on education could bring the Church into conflict with the government over the ownership of schools rather than over 'the important aspects of the school curriculum and the extent of religion as a constitutional right'.[66]

Tanner's observations were prophetic. Before six months elapsed, the Church in Rhodesia was engaged in conflict with government over ownership and administration of schools. Perhaps, it is appropriate to say that the Church was caught unawares: this is the reason why the Government's new education policy created the anxiety that it did among missionaries. There had been complacency regarding the Church school previously. That could explain Tanner's apparent disillusionment during his one-month visit to Rhodesia. After completing his survey he wrote:

> There seems to be a widespread feeling that it is not worth having ideas — they are not asked for and when they are proffered, they are not used .... Thus change, if it comes at all, appears to encroach on the people more from outside rather than as a result of their own discussions and ideas.[67]

True, change finally encroached on the Church from outside. The new education policy brought about a crisis in the Church leadership and hence the conflict of opinion on what action to take. Ultimately the Church had to relinquish authority over the schools.

The hand-over of schools started at the beginning of 1971. In 1972, 975 primary schools, with a total enrolment of 149 000 pupils were handed over to local councils or to the central government. Only 75 schools, with a pupil enrolment of 23 439 remained in the hands of the Church. These 75 schools were located on mission farms and were to be retained by the Church. There were two reasons for this retention. Firstly, after consulting the laity and clergy at both Catholic Association and Pastoral Council levels, the bishops decided 'to meet in some degree the wishes of the people' to retain the schools. Secondly, the Bishops retained the schools as a practical measure to avoid 'disadvantages that would seem to attach to the operation on one site of a church authority and another authority (that is, Council ) in charge of a school'.[70]

## The immediate results of the loss of schools

The immediate implications of the loss of schools by the Church can be classified into two, the positive and negative.

### *Negative implications*

The loss of schools from Church control was seen by some rural Catholic parents as negative because it brought a more irksome financial burden on them. As mentioned earlier, some children were forced to drop out of the school because of increased fees called for in both government sponsored and council schools.[72]

Some missionaries saw the loss of schools as 'tragic'. No longer were they certain of having a steady increase in the number of Catholics. All that was now undermined. The new situation was potentially dangerous since the future of mission was now unpredictable.[74]

## Positive implications

The loss of schools posed a threat to the constant growth of the Church, but to a large extent that loss also provided a challenge for new thinking on approaches to evangelisation. Rather than mourn the loss, some priests found occasion to assess the value of the schools that the church had considered indispensable. At a Seminar at Oxford, Fr Paul Edwards challenged the viability and efficacy of the school system that the Church had clung to for decades. He noted that:

> At a time when Education is regarded by Africans as the 'open sesame' to the paradise of this world, it is hardly surprising if Christianity, the almost necessary concomitant to education, should be accepted. Also it is not surprising if it should be as easily abandoned again once one has gone as far as possible on the education band-waggon.[75]

Or, in the words of Bishop C. Alderson of the Anglican province of Mashonaland, 'the African people wanted education and the Church provided it, seeing it as sugar around the pill of Christianity'.[76]

According to Fr. Edwards, the loss of schools was necessary as it forced the Church to distinguish between education as a way of 'getting on in the world,' and Christianity.[77] He thus viewed the loss of primary schools as a development that had a potential to 'revolutionise our African apostolate'.[78]

More significantly though, the loss of schools was bound to transform the dual role of the lay teacher. The change of responsibility from the Church to local council or central government became some sort of empowerment for lay teachers who had felt compelled to teach Catholic doctrine without being given latitude to choose. As the hand-over took effect, lay teachers were afforded room to be true to themselves and to decide freely if they wanted to be responsible for Catholic children in their charge as an act of 'living the faith and witnessing to it rather than being paid for it, or looking up to the priest for job promotion'.[79]

Naturally, the relationship between the priest and the teacher changed too. The priest could now be approached in precisely his role as priest and not as an employer, teacher or manager. The priest was freed from administrative work in connection with the schools. This created new opportunities for more fruitful involvement in pastoral work.[80] Stripped of his power as employer the priest could approach the school teacher more easily on neutral ground.[81]

## Conclusion

The hand-over of primary schools to other responsible authorities did not simply affect the relations between the priests and the teaching profession; it affected the very missionary approach of the Church in Zimbabwe. In one priest's view the change meant that the Church needed to concern itself with:

> all sectors of the population rather than with children alone. The Church had to learn to rely on the African apostolate that would be the only assurance for its future.[82]

The schools' crisis accentuated rather than mitigated the need to keep abreast with theological thinking on ministerial priesthood in the universal Church. The Rhodesian church, still largely expatriate in its operations, was forced to move on to 'a clarified concept of the priesthood in terms of the priest's central functions, as opposed to his non-essential functions'.[83] According to N. Weeks, the strictly sacerdotal function of priests and bishops involved presiding over local Christian communities and the celebration of the Eucharist.[84]

But considering the untenable ratio of priests to the Catholic population, which stood at 1 to 1 200, it became necessary to fill, by other methods and ministries the gaps left by teachers who withdrew from teaching Catholic doctrine[85]. There was much to do if growth in Catholic population was to be realised. The ratio of priests to the whole population, standing at 1 to 14 400, had to be balanced by more vocations or by other ministries, including the recognition of the laity. Clearly new models had to be developed, away from the school. This will be the concern of the next chapter.

## Notes

1. Skelton, K, *Bishop in Smith's Rhodesia*, p.103.
2. Randolph, *Church and State in Rhodesia: 1969–1971*, p.76.
3. Ibid.
4. Ibid., p.68.
5. Dachs, A J and Rea, W F, *The Catholic Church and Zimbabwe (1879–1979)*, p.146.

CHAPTER 3 — *Church Renewal and Challenges from the Minority Regime*  39

6. *Ibid.,* p.167.
7. *Ibid.,* p.181.
8. Rhodesian Catholic Bishop Conference Newsletter, No. 217, April, 1972, p.2.
9. *Ibid.*
10. *Ibid.,* p3.
11. Interview with Mr S Mushandu, a member of the Wesleyan Methodist Church. His children attended Chesvingo Catholic School under Serima Mission. All of them had to become Catholic. Interview at his farm in Lancashire, Chivhu, 17 October, 1991.
12 Callaghan, E, "The Teaching of Religion", Oxford Seminar Report, p.17 [Jesuit Archives, Cf. file on the Oxford Seminar]
13. Doba, E, former Headteacher of Chesvingo primary school, Interview, 12 Nov. 1992.
14. Alois Banda, former Boarding master of Mukaro primary school. Interview, 16 Oct. 1992.
15. *Ibid.*
16. Fr Hubmann of Mukaro Mission. Interview, 4 Oct. 1991.
17. Randolph, *op cit.,* p.68. cf New Education Act, 1967, pp. 3, 4 and 5.
18. Randolph, Interview 22 September, 1988 at Prestage House Harare.
19. Grant, G C, *The Africans' Predicament in Rhodesia,* report No. 8., Minority Rights Group, p.10. cf. Hansard, 23 Sept 1969.
20. *Ibid.*
21. Randolph, *op.cit.,* p.71.
22. Randolph, interview, cf. note 18.
23. Paul Edwards "Implications for the church of recent developments in Rhodesia." pp. 16, 19. cf. note 12.
24. Skelton, *op.cit.,* p.103.
25. Rhodesia Catholic Bishops' Conference, Newsletter, No. 21, April, 1972 p. 13.
26. Burrough, J, *Angels Unawares,* p.67. Also cf. E McDonagh *The Demands of Simple Justice,* p.70.
27. Grant, *op.cit.,* p.10. See also Randolph, *op.cit.,* p.69.
28. Skelton, *op.cit,* p.104.
29. *Ibid.*
30. Randolph, *op.cit.,* p.66.
31. Best, A G, & de Blig J, *African Survey,* 299.
32. Supra, p.48.
33. Elsener J, 'The Missionary and Socio-Economic Action, Mambo Press', Oxford Seminar, p.54.
34 *Ibid.*

35. *Ibid.*
36. Haene, A, Interview, at Driefontein on 14 February, 1991.
37. *Ibid.*
38. Elsener, *op.cit.*
39. *Ibid.*
40. Edwards, P, 'Implications for the church of recent developments in Rhodesia'. p.17. Cf. note 23.
41. Sr Gemma Chifamba (ZCBC) — (Catholic Secretariat) Interview at the Catholic Secretariat on 3 July, 1990. Teacher and later Secretary for Education (Harare Archdiocese Archives).
42. *Ibid.*
43. Linden, *Church and State in Rhodesia*, pp.102 and 104.
44. Supra, p.47.
45. Bishop, D, Lamont, quoted in Elsener's paper, *op.cit.*, p.54.
46. Randolph, *Report to Rome* p.46.
47. Linden, *op.cit.*, p.86.
48. RCBC, Newsletter No. 21, April 1972, p.13.
49. Supra, pp. 44–45.
50. 1968 Education Statistics, Pastoral Centre, Harare.
51. Fr Pascal Slevin — Wedza, He was Headmaster of Mt St Mary's from 1964 till 1981 and Parish priest up to 1995.
52. Fr Pascal Slevin, Interview, at Mt. St Mary's on 16 Oct. 1991.
53. Tanner (memo 15), p.3. cf. Ch.2, note 40.
54. Randolph, *Report to Rome*, p.49.
55. *Ibid*, p. 45.
56. Mr Tome, Headmaster of Mt St Mary's Secondary School. Interview 26 October, 1990.
57. Mahuni, H/M of Murezi Primary School 1990–20 Sept 1992. Interview at Murezi on 20 September, 1990.
58. Edwards, *op.cit*, p.17.
59. *Ibid.*
60. Callaghan, E, 'The Teaching of Religion,' Oxford Seminar p.57. Cf. note 33.
61. Slevin Fr Paschal, cf. note 52.
62. Best, *op.cit.*, p.128.
63. Tanner, R, Memo 15, (Education Bias), p.3. cf. note 53. (Jesuit Archives)
64. *Ibid.*

65. Ibid.
66. Ibid., p.2.
67. Tanner, R, Memo 3, (Change), points 3 and 4 cf. note 63.
68. RCBC Newsletter, No.27, October 1972, p.17.
69. Edwards, op.cit, p.17.
70. Ibid.
71. Chikuvire, P, who had five children going to primary school. Interview 18 March, 1992 at Chivhu.
72. Chigwedere, (Chivhu) First Council Secretary of Lancashire Purchase area. The Council ran 5 schools. Interview 17 June, 1991 at Chivhu.
73. Edwards, op.cit, p.17.
74. Fr K Spence, Education Secretary for the Salisbury diocese then. Interview 17 Sept 1988 at Prestage House.
75. Edwards, op.cit.
76. Skelton, op.cit.
77. Edwards, op.cit.
78. Ibid., p.12.
79. Chadya, C, teacher at Mt St Mary's Wedza. Interview, 28 October, 1990.
80. RCBC Newsletter No.21, April, 1972, p.15.
81. Edwards, op.cit.
82. Fr W Nyatsanza, Gweru diocese, Interviewed on 17 August, 1990.
83. Weeks, N, 'What is the local Church? The role of the priest', Oxford Seminar papers, p.26 cf. note 40.
84. Ibid.
85. According to Bishop P Mutume many teachers quit teaching Catholic doctrine as soon as the Church surrendered the schools to councils. This became a matter of concern to the Church. Interview — 16 September, 1991 at the Catholic Secretariat.

# Chapter 4

# The 'Local Church' and Local Political Mobilisation

## Introduction
Developments in the educational field since 1969 forced the Church to reconsider its strategy for evangelism. Political developments reinforced the need for contextual appropriation of the teaching of the Second Vatican Council on the 'local Church' and basic Christian communities. Continued attempts to implement the new eccelesiology had to interact with the heightened political mobilisation at grassroots level, which was a spontaneous response in critique of attempts to reach a settlement which would give the Smith regime its badly needed international recognition. In this process the Catholic African Association took on itself a new role which ran parallel to the African National Council, on the Protestant side. This development was from 1971 to 1975.

## Continued problems with the concept of parish
As already illustrated from the mid-1960's the new Catholic thinking on the parish as 'the living cell' and 'the ecclesial community organised locally', with the pastor as its minister proved to be increasingly contested.[1] The canonical notion of parish became untenable especially in the rural situation, where, for example:

> 'one mission station which is canonically a parish covers an area of 10 000 square kilometres, populated by 55 000 people, of whom only 900 are Catholics, some of them living 150 kilometres apart'.[2]

This was the case in the rural diocese of Wankie and in this diocese, as in any others, Catholics of the same rural parish seldom had a chance to meet. The many outstations set up over the decades around the central mission station had not evolved into independent parishes because of shortage of priests. The parish therefore was made up of unconnected groups, which had very little in common except their Catholic faith.[3] Clearly, these parishioners could never be said to constitute a community in a truly ecclesial sense.

CHAPTER 4 — *The 'Local Church' and Local Political Mobilisation* 43

By the mid-1960's, when church-owned primary schools were still very much at the center of the church evangelisation, many sparsely populated groups of Catholics, living away from both the mission station and the school, went for over a month without having received any pastoral visit from the parish priest.[4] Needless to say such out stations went for over a month without receiving the Eucharist. Yet the presence of the church-run primary schools in itself meant a lot for those people who provided neighbourhood to them. Instead of walking long distances to the mission centre for mass they joined the church service of school pupils on a week day when the priest visited the school. However, these infrequent visits were not enough to create vibrant and committed Catholics. The crisis of the parish could only be averted through the adoption of alternative pastoral and ecclesiological models.

## Training full-time catechists and financial stringency from Rome

Cognisant of the shortage of priests in catering for the pastoral needs of their parishioners, the Rhodesian Bishops had in 1963 decided to adopt and support the Wankie diocese's proven Catechist training programme. The Rhodesia Bishops' Conference decided to take over Matetsi in Wankie and confer on it the status of a National Catechetical School.[5] From 1963 to 1972, this school turned out ninety four full-time lay catechists, who having undergone two years of scriptural, theological and catechetical training, joined their priests in order to nurture a vibrant local Church in Zimbabwe.[6]

One major problem with the programme to train fulltime catechists, however, was its dependence on external support. The old adage is still true that he who pays the piper calls the tune. We have already observed in Chapter Two a direct expression of this problem. The National Catechetical School at Matetsi depended on support from the Sacred Congregation for the Evangelisation of the Peoples in Rome. Moreover, graduates of the school who went back to work in parishes were paid from grants from the same source in Rome. And up to 1970 these grants came to Rhodesia annualy.[7]

However, a change of policy in Rome directly affected the programme in Rhodesia. From 1969, Rome decided to gradually phase out the support for the catechist training programme and the payment of salaries to the catechists in parishes. In early 1970, the Secretary General of the Congregation for the Evangelisation of Peoples in Rome unequivocally reiterated the need for reorienting the church in Rhodesia to be more supportive of its catechists. Responding to a request for support by the

Rhodesia Catholic Bishops' Conference, Bishop Conway of the Congregation for the Evangelisation of Peoples replied:

> For the good of the local church, it is desirable that the principle of responsibility and self-sufficiency in material needs be encouraged. Otherwise we support a parasitical church.[8]

This was the message that the bishops in Rhodesia had to preach to their flock. They had to appeal to their constituency to change and become more involved in their own Church affairs at the local level. At a meeting on religious teaching held on 23 February 1971, Archbishop Francis Markall had to repeat a statement he already had made when discussing the payment of catechists.[9] Rome's new policy was that the money to pay catechists and to finance catechetical work had to be raised from the dioceses and the parishes. Rome would contribute a very small fraction of the amount needed. Archbishop Markall went further: 'We must aim at helping and supporting our own catechetical work more and more and even gradually becoming independent of outside aid.[10]

The Sacred Congregation for the Evangelisation of Peoples earmarked the grants they sent to Rhodesia for 'the training of catechetical workers and highly qualified pastoral workers'.[11] The latter were expected to produce catechetical books, teach religion in universities and other centers of higher education and supervise the work of catechists. It was this class of highly educated pastoral workers that Rome regarded as the future backbone of evangelisation in the church.

Rome also advised the bishops to place new emphasis on the training of 'religious leaders and community leaders that is, people who practically carry out all the duties of a pastor except those functions which require ordination'.[12] These religious leaders had to be 'community leaders in the sense that they had to be farmers or craftsmen, who by conscientious work at their farming or their trades, offered a good example to others.'[13] Such community leaders, Rome noted, with their Christian witness might be better accepted if they worked as volunteers rather than as paid catechists.[14]

The bishops and pastoral planners in the Church in Rhodesia had no option but to go by Rome's advice. It was beyond doubt that without Rome's support the dioceses could not afford employing paid fulltime catechists. Therefore, primarily, for financial reasons, voluntary part-time catechists were viewed as the only viable lay ministers for the Church. These at least could be within the support capacity of the grassroots local communities, if need be.[15] One thing that parish priests hated was to levy tax on parishioners in order to support full-time catechists. Moreover these trained catechists would be the best starting point in the process of stimulating the basic Christian communities in leadership responsibility and faith. Only then would voluntary catechists emerge.[16] Meanwhile the National Catechetical School at Matetsi, Wankie, was made to wind up its work. Up to 1970 seventy three catechists had graduated from it, sixty-eight laymen, two laywomen and three sisters. The Bishops' Conference recommended that it should have its last intake in 1972. In this last intake, twenty-one candidates were enrolled.[17]

As we have seen already the Church's problems in the late sixties and early seventies were based on the inadequate supply of priests. There was an over dependence on expatriate priests, who from 1950 to 1970 had increased from 125 to 314.[18] However, by the early 1970's, a good number of these priests were ageing. Unfortunately there were no replacements available due to the general shortage of vocations in Europe.[19] Local vocations to the priesthood were more numerous in the diocese of Gwelo than any others, but even there they were not sufficient to replace the number of expatriate priests who died or had to retire because of old age or illness.[20] From 1950 to 1970, there was also an increase in the number of indigenous clergy from 3 to 34, but this was a desperately slow growth rate when related to the actual need.[21] Meanwhile from 1950 to 1970 the Catholic membership had increased from 76 139 to 475 374. A comparison of the clergy to laity ratio between 1950 and 1970 shows that the situation was degenerating. In 1970 it had become 1:1 267 while in 1950 it was 1:594. Even so such a ratio does not give us a true picture of the situation since the aging clergy had to be allocated less burdensome work and short hours for pastoral visits.

The training of indigenous clergy was also affected by the budget-tightening policies in Rome. Although the Regional (National) Seminary at Chishawasha enrolled the highest numbers of seminarians in 1970 compared to any other year, the Bishops' Conference viewed the support from Rome as 'wholly inadequate'. They decided therefore that from 1970 each bishop was going to provide for the support of the seminarians out of his 'ordinary' subsidy.[22] This new system brought with it inequalities among the Seminarians leading to substantial discontent which often exploded in the forms of strikes or class boycotts at the seminary. These often led to suspensions and expulsions or withdrawal of some seminarians.[23]

According to Rev Dr T. Jakata, the question of young men going to the Seminary for largely secular reasons may have influenced Rome's policy. In his opinion, however, the change of policy did not yield better results for the Church:

> In the short term, Rome's financial policies had negative rather than positive impact on indigenous vocation. We can even say the same for the long term, because we have not yet realised a substantial change (upsurge) since the early 1970's.[24]

If the Bishops were to chart new and locally viable pastoral programmes it was necessary for them to be in control of the finances in their dioceses. As yet, due to the missionary structures in operation, more money was being received by religious superiors of religious institutes than by the bishops. In 1970, all bishops in Rhodesia were members of religions institutes. The bishops, or parish priests like former mission superiors, relied on the religious superiors for operational finances.[25] It was only in 1970 when Rome reduced the support that had been a major source of direct finance to bishops, that the latter saw the need to regulate the inflow of money from missionary institutes and other sources of the religious regional superiors and mission superiors. The Rhodesia Bishops' Conference decided henceforth to include a regulatory caveat in the contract between the diocese and missionary institutes in order for the bishop to be aware of the new regulations.[26]

The relinquishing of schools, which was discussed in the previous chapter, added to a far greater negative impact on the evangelisation of the Church than the financial controls that Rome was exerting. As we have already indicated, in the ten years that the National Catechetical School trained full time catechists for the country only about one hundred had graduated from it.[27] With the schools the issue was totally different. The schools had remained the backbone of missionary evangelisation since the early days of the missionary Church in Zimbabwe, and especially from 1948 when the government was persuaded to share responsibility for African education by paying teacher's salaries.[28] The fact that the school rather than the Church remained the locus of missionary thinking up to the 1970's showed , not only a lack of pastoral foresight, but also political confidence in the colonial governments. Whatever criticism the Africans had of colonialism, the church viewed it as benevolent and could therefore continue to rally close to the colonial establishment, not just for safety but also to ensure the spread of the Gospel and the social services it envisaged. Apart from being biased towards school-going youth at the expense of the adults, and being left in the hands of the teacher at the expense of the parents, the Church school was 'not enlivened by kerygmatic preaching and popular liturgy'.[29]

Although primary schools were surrendered to local councils from 1971, the Catholic clergy were of the opinion that Catholic teachers would continue teaching catechism and leading Sunday services without priests. Unfortunately this hope turned to a disappointment when many teachers gave up the regular practice of their faith. In 1971 and 1972, the Catechetical commission, which had introduced the Right-of-Entry in schools surrendered to local councils found out that when schools were handed

## CHAPTER 4 — The 'Local Church' and Local Political Mobilisation

over to Council administration only 10 per cent of the near 6 000 Catholic teachers were willing to take part in Catechetical training.[30] This disinterest in matters of faith by Catholic teachers created anxious moments for the Church leadership because teachers had become the heads of the emerging groups of Christians, as well as the indispensable link between the missionary and the people.[31]

The Right-of-Entry, which literally meant the right of churches to teach religion to their Church members or catechumens at the schools which were secularised, could only take off if adult lay members were prepared to shoulder the responsibility to teach the faith to their young ones. The disinterest of Catholic teachers in teaching the Right-of-Entry pushed the Church to explore new approaches of evangelising of the young.

One evidence of this is the conference in 1970 which was attended by the bishops of Rhodesia and the executives of both the newly founded Conferences of Major Religious Superiors and Major Superiors of Women Religious (CMRS and CMSWR). At this conference a resolution was passed calling for diversification of pastoral methods and approaches. The church leaders emphasised the importance of moving away from institutions and recommended the need to concentrate on non-institutional work like leadership training, adult instruction and education, and a concerted apostolic involvement of the laity.[32] The Church leaders envisaged a better chance of survival once they had given up their traditional institutional work.[33]

While the Church leadership resolved to try alternative pastoral methods and approaches, one burning issue was the teaching of the faith to the Catholic children in local council schools using the so-called Right-of-Entry.[34] The Bishops' Conference had delegated parish priests to organise and approve of fit persons to teach. These persons could be religious brothers, sisters, teachers, competent catechists or suitable lay persons.[35]

Depending on the availability of suitable persons to teach the Right-of-Entry classes, each diocese was left to its own devices. Wankie diocese, which had been in the forefront in the training of full-time catechists, decided to deploy its ready resource of fulltime catechists to local council schools.[36] Umtali and Gwelo dioceses relied on trained teachers, who apparently had not abandoned catechetical teaching in large numbers as in other dioceses.[37] The diocese of Bulawayo resorted to sisters while that of Salisbury thought of the Catholic African Association more than any other Catholic grouping. We will consider the Archdiocese of Salisbury's programme in considerable detail, in order to evaluate the contribution that the Catholic African Association made towards the nurturing of thousands of young Catholics attending school in local council schools.

## The Catholic Association, 1970-74

Drawing on the strength and apostolic role of the Catholic African Association (CAA) in the Archdiocese of Salisbury, Bishop Markall, in 1970, challenged the Association's members to play a crucial role in the future life of the church. He wrote:

> In view of the added importance which is given to the organisation of the pastoral side of our work, consequent upon the forcible surrender of the management of our primary schools, the work of the CAA is at an even higher priority than before.[38]

Before sending out the letter from which the above quotation is part, the bishop had sent out an *Ad Clerum* asking all spiritual directors to the CAA to attend a meeting to consider ways in which the Church could maximise the pastoral work of the Association.[39]

The meeting on 23 June 1970, presided over by Archbishop Markall, passed a resolution that the CAA be asked to assist in catechetical work in the council schools. Secondly, a call was made for prominent CAA members to avail themselves for election into the local council boards. This could create avenues through which the CAA could influence the new situation with Christian principles. The parish priests and spiritual advisers attending this meeting felt that once a Christian impression was made at the council board level, the interests of the Church in the rural areas would be safeguarded.[40] This meeting emphasised the need to make full use of the apostolate of the laity as required by the Second Vatican Council. The Bishop referred specifically to the teachings that empower the laity:

> The laity are given a special vocation to make the church present and fruitful in those places and circumstances where it is only through them that she can become the salt of the earth.[41]

The participants also resolved that a one-day course be organised at Silveira House, which would acquaint leaders of the CAA with the aims, structure, function and financing of local councils.[42]

In spite of the confidence that the Archbishop and the priests attending this meeting had in the CAA, it did not occur to them that CAA leadership could have been invited to the meeting. At this meeting, the Archbishop and his priests, on their own, decided to chart the future of a church which was henceforth to rely heavily on the laity.

The Archbishop and priests of Salisbury archdiocese had good reasons for rating the Catholic African Association so highly, above all other lay organisations in the diocese. The CAA in the Archdiocese had not posed any serious problems nor had come in conflict with other lay organisations at a time that the church leadership had called for the setting up of parish Council.[43] The CAA in the Salisbury Archdiocese 'had shown commitment to creating Catholic opinion by assisting the penetration of Catholic faith into every sphere of peoples' lives'.[44] Clearly, the Archbishop had confidence in the CAA.

The CAA in the Salisbury Archdiocese had emerged from the doldrums of the anti-church nationalistic zeal in the mid-sixties, to become a powerful organisation. From 1968 to 1970, its paid-up membership was running above 3 000, a membership complement unequalled before.[45]

From mid-1970 to about the end of 1971, the CAA rendered distinguished service in evangelization in the diocese by way of teaching Right-of-Entry lessons in primary schools and teaching catechism.[46] However, one event, which was to become of crucial importance to the black people of Zimbabwe, undermined the hope that the Church had in the CAA. This event was the 1971 constitutional talks between the British Government and the Rhodesian Front Government, the Home-Smith proposals for majority rule. The CAA was one of the internal organisations asked to give its opinion on the merits and demerits of the proposed internal settlement. It set up an *ad hoc* committee to study the settlement proposals for submission to CAA. Territorial Executive. The three member committee, advised by Dr Edison Sithole, concluded that the Home-Smith proposals would produce a constitution that was to 'remain very much the same as the 1969 Constitution in character'.[47] Such a constitution, they further argued, was highly faulty because much depended 'on the goodwill of government . . . At any rate, the questions of party and even majority rule seem to be a very long term dream'.[48] The CAA *ad hoc* Committee advised the CAA Territorial Executive, on 7 December 1971, to say 'no' to the Home-Smith settlement proposals.[49]

Henceforth, the CAA leadership, which at this time was predominantly constituted by members from the Salisbury Archdiocese, embarked on a campaign to mobilise Catholics against the Internal Settlement. They visited parishes, giving talks throughout the country, but especially in Salisbury and Umtali dioceses where the CAA was still alive.[50] This political campaign left the CAA in open conflict with most of the missionary parish priests who were invariably the CAA spiritual fathers. Most of them did not welcome the openly political stance which the association had taken.[51] To the CAA leaders and members, the efforts of these priests to prevent the parish members from discussing the proposals were interpreted as signaling the priests' support of the Rhodesian whites, the majority of whom had voted for 'the repressive and discriminatory 1969 Constitution'.[52]

But for the CAA leadership, the mere fact that the CAA was asked to give its opinion about the Home-Smith settlement proposals was viewed as a recognition of the popularity it enjoyed among the African population:

> If the British recognised the CAA, who were the priests to deny us the right to educate the church on the implications of the Home-Smith proposals for a new Constitution. We were prepared to fight the spiritual fathers who were against majority rule. With or without their permission and presence, we were determined to teach all Catholics of the evils of these proposals.[53]

It is within this political context in Salisbury Archdiocese that the relationship between parish councils and the CAA became characterised by antagonism rather than cooperation from the early 1970's. Many European priests understood the CAA as being interested in usurping the functions of the newly formed parish councils.[54]

However, there were a good number of parishes where the CAA still undertook such a function because there were not yet any parish councils. The CAA did not cease to operate, even when a parish council was formed. Failure to disband became the cause of great misunderstanding in some places.[55]

From the beginning of 1972, signs of polarisation between the CAA and missionary priests were on the increase. There was growing resentment especially against the white spiritual directors appointed by the Archbishop. This resentment led the CAA leadership of the Salisbury region to request the Archbishop to appoint African spiritual directors. Members of the CAA pointed out to the Archbishop that 'some spiritual directors (Europeans) did not want the CAA' The Archbishop, however, would not hear of this, arguing that, 'that would be tantamount to having an African Catholic Church, and many European spiritual fathers may not entertain the idea'.[56]

As already stated above, it is apparent that the mere fact of having been consulted on the Home-Smith proposals had major symbolic significance to the CAA. The Home-Smith settlement proposals which were rejected by the majority Africans had left a mark of self-worth in the Association, and affirmed the dignity of Africans in general. The CAA in particular seems to have stressed the need for dialogue and consultation more eloquently after 1971.

Evidence of this was when the Archbishop in 1972 decided to form three independent CAA, (henceforth CA), regions out of the archdiocese. This was in line with his future plan to establish the episcopal vicariates of Marandellas and Sinoia, to fall under the jurisdiction of the Irish Franciscans and the German Jesuits respectively. The rest of Salisbury diocese would therefore remain the domain of English Jesuits.[57] This subdivision of the

Archdiocese meant that each CA region was to engage in activities on its own since the subdivision made them independent units. As a result, the operation of the CA was directly affected. In August 1972, each jurisdiction held a congress. One was held at Wedza (Marandellas), another at Banket (Archdiocese) and yet another at Kutama (Sinoia). The vicar of Marandellas, without consulting the Regional CA had asked the CA members in his jurisdiction to set up an interim executive committee.[58]

While the Archbishop's plan of decentralisation may have been carried out to benefit the whole diocese, in reality it did substantial damage to the co-ordinated operation of the CA At the CA regional meeting in December, the majority of representatives expressed misgivings about the move by the Archbishop. They objected most strongly to the decentralisation, which they viewed as reflecting racial prejudices within foreign missionary groups. The subdivision of the diocese, they further argued, left the CA fragmented and consequently at the mercy of the powerful missionary groupings. This was viewed as leading to the ultimate demise of the Catholic Association. The representatives at this meeting were highly critical of the Archbishop's implementation of his plan without consulting the laity, and especially the CA.[59]

In 1973, there were many reports of inactivity of the Catholic Association in many parts of the archdiocese. The reasons given for this inactivity focussed more on the authoritarian attitude of the clergy than on the organisational failure of the CA leadership. The members of the CA complained of 'lack of support from the spiritual fathers who only think of the CA as a money collecting organisation for the support of priests'.[60]

The CA realised that it was part of its duty to maintain parish priests, but the problem was rather that of inadequate consultation and communication between the clergy and the CA laypersons. Tensions between the CA and the priests often arose because the parish priests 'introduced new ideas to the parish before having properly studied the situation'.[61] The CA leadership also expressed strong dissatisfaction especially with the way the reform of the liturgy was being introduced by priests into the church services without enough consultation having been made with the faithful.[62]

The period between 1968 and 1974 was characterised by experiments in the liturgy, especially the introduction of liturgical songs, gestures and the funerary rites. Apparently these experiments were undertaken without much consultation and debate among the laity, hence the conflicts.

In this period too, the CA, supported by its long-standing regional spiritual adviser, Fr M Hannan, started to question the appointment of the CA spiritual advisers at the parish levels by the hierarchy. The official appointments, the members argued, left the CA without 'real power to run its own affairs'.

To their knowledge, other societies, like St Vincent de Paul, had whole responsibility over their affairs, but they were not working in conflict with the parish priests.[63] It was felt that the appointment of the spiritual directors by the Archbishop gave the former undue power over the Catholic Association branches. Because of this, a spiritual director, who was invariably the parish priest, could ban the CA in his parish. For instance:

> A parish priest for Mabvuku wrote to the CA Chairman for Mabvuku parish board banning the CA and asking the CA board to give their bank book and all money collected by the CA to the executive committee of the parish council there.[64]

The parish board secretary referred the matter to the regional secretary who in turn referred the matter to the Archdiocese's auxiliary bishop, Rev P F Chakaipa, who was then the only African prelate.[65] That the conflict between the CA membership and parish priests had assumed unprecedented levels of power wrangling is confirmed by one last example that we will give. At a regional congress at Musami in August 1974 Fr M Hannan noted that 'one of the priests with charge of souls deliberately organised a retreat for women so that the women could not go to the CA congress'.[66]

Father Hannan went on to observe that:

> One of the women who attended the retreat and then made her way to the congress professed that she would probably have her *chita* (League of Mary) garments confiscated by the priest in question for attending the congress.[67]

Incidentally it was Bishop P F Chakaipa who was officially opening the congress. As a result of these conflicts, the CA in the Archdiocese made little progress in the catechetical work and in Right-of-Entry classes. The new political circumstances of the early seventies created an awareness in the members which the missionary priests viewed as inimical to the growth and operations of the Church. The totalitarian tendencies in the clergy did not afford the CA leadership and membership the environment to operate freely and lead the Church to new heights. As the CA was being bombarded by authoritarian pressures in the Church, Moto magazine, its own brainchild was being subjected to government pressure too. Moto was banned in September 1974, first for three months and later, permanently up 1979. It was only during the ceasefire that Lord Soames lifted the ban on 21 December 1979.[68]

## Alternative models of evangelisation

The disinterest of the Catholic teachers in teaching Catholic religion in council schools across the country, and the failure of the Catholic Association to fill the vacuum, created a crisis in the Church's programme of evangelisation. The teachers and the Catholic Association were products of the Church's programme towards creating an elite, that was meant to further the evangelisation of the African people in more effective ways than by the European missionaries.[69] However, nothing substantial was allowed to come out of these two African elite groups. While Archbishop F Markall of Salisbury was trying to get the best out of the Catholic Association, some parish priests in his diocese were busy experimenting with other non-elitist models of evangelisation. We will refer to some such models that, we argue, provided an alternative and appropriate model of evangelisation in Zimbabwe.

## The urban parish

The shortage of priests was a problem for both the rural and urban Church. The urban Church was equally affected by the decision from Rome, which reduced the external financing of catechetical training and support.[70] The need for reformulation of pastoral methods and approaches was more compelling for urban parishes like St Peters, Harare, than it was in many rural areas.[71]

From the early sixties, urban parishes, like Harare and Highfield in Salisbury and Mpopoma and Pumula in Bulawayo, experienced unprecedented influxes of youths coming from the country seeking employment. Most of these job seekers had attended school and achieved various levels at either primary or secondary levels.[72] This influx not only adversely affected the social amenities of the towns but also stretched the ratio of the priest to parishioners.

The spiritual needs of many parishioners could not be met by the few priests who manned urban parishes. The one or two catechists who acted as the priests' assistants did not make much difference under the changing circumstances. Urban parishes like the ones named above were undergoing a crisis of identity. The parish priest could no longer manage the parish, while the parishioners could no longer feel adequately ministered to.[73] Innovative parish priests, conscious of their inadequacies in meeting the needs of parishioners embarked on pastoral programmes based on co-responsibility between laity and clergy. Two urban models were embarked upon, one at St Antony's parish in Bulawayo under Fr Alexander Alapont, and the other at St Peter's parish in Salisbury under Fr Wim Smulders. We will briefly discuss the St Peter's model because its success later became a great motivation for what became a nationally approved pastoral strategy.

## St Peter's pastoral programme (1969-73)

In 1969, Fr Wim Smulders, with his associate at St Peter's, Fr Antony Bex, realised that it was impractical for them even remotely to get to all their parishioners on an organised system of visiting. It was no longer viable to take the parish as a whole as one community. The situation was worsened by the fact that St Peter's parish now had two churches, St Peter's (Old Church) and St Peter's (New Church), the latter completed in 1965.[74] The new church was built as a response to the expansion of the Harare suburb, which from the early sixties was experiencing unprecedented increases in population.[75]

The two priests observed that the contact that they were making with their parishioners was too irregular or if regular 'far too widely spaced in time to be of great value'.[76] The parishioners could hardly feel contact with the parish, if this were the means of approaching their lives and problems.[77]

Realising the crisis of identity that the parish was undergoing, Frs Smulders and Bex decided to divide it up into community clusters or neighbourhood clusters. The priests gradually went round all the clusters with a member of the parish council saying mass in the home of a willing parishioner[78]. After some time there emerged a 'tightly knit little community of about ten streets each or three blocks of hostels'.[79] These communities became known as 'Sections' of the parish, and twenty-four of them came into existence.[80]

The priests promoted within each 'section' the holding of evening prayer meetings. At first, the members met only once a week but in due course the frequency increased to three times or more.[81] At these prayer meetings, the 'section' members met not only to pray but also to share reflections on Biblical passages and themes. One motivating factor was that the New Testament in Shona had just been printed in 1968. This translation was enthusiastically received in the sections. Through it, the Holy Scripture was brought within easy reach of the faithful. This development made the St Peter's evening prayers in the homes of the faithful really vibrant.

One member of St. Peter's church reminisced:

> Meeting as lay persons to share our own reflections on the Bible was a novel but very exciting development. As women at our Sodalities we could do so but this time it was not a women's affair, it was like to a mini-church. Everybody was so enthusiastic about the new changes. And naturally during the early phase we often met for much longer than we intended.[82]

Although traditionally St Peter's had six members constituting the executive of the parish council the division of the parish into sections brought about the need officially to recognise new ecclesial structures.

CHAPTER 4 — *The 'Local Church' and Local Political Mobilisation*      55

It soon became clear that there should be leaders in each section, as well known at section level as the parish executive at parish level.[83]

With time, many tasks that used to be handled by the priest and the parish executive devolved on to the sections and their leaders. The section leadership gradually gained more and more stature as they became:

> consultants and indisputable advisers to the priests. When it came to baptising, marrying, taking children for religious courses, receiving catechumens or organising funerals, the priests necessarily had to consult the section leaders.[84]

Pastorally, the zone and section model proved to be very effective. Each section became 'more and more a family where prayer and care were keynotes of the faith'.[85] The sections, unlike the formerly centralized parish, were personal and more parental in image. In the sections:

> no one can say that he feels out of things, unknown and with no one to turn to. All can come with their problems, which are dealt with at whatever level is required, or desired by the person concerned.[86]

The model evolved at St Peter's proved to be a very successful experiment which other parishes, in both urban and rural areas, emulated and adapted to their specific needs. Parishes in Salisbury like Old and New Highfield, Glen Norah, Kambuzuma-Rugare and Mabvuku-Tafara, because of their proximity to St Peter's, adopted the model before rural parishes did.[87] However, because the whole country was interested in developing alternative pastoral models, the St Peter's model quickly found its way to the National Pastoral Centre, and from the Pastoral Centre to other parishes in the country in form of disseminated pastoral information. The setting up of the national Pastoral Centre was another result of the pastoral restructuring influenced by Vatican II. The conference of Major Religious Superios, established in November, 1969 impressed upon the Bishops the need to set up a Pastoral Centre whose functions would be, among others, to co-ordinate and develop a pastoral programme of renewal.

The most urgent need was considered to be the updating of the clergy and the strengthening of collaboration between the hierarchy, the clergy and laity. The recommendations of the CMRS were accepted by the bishops and in March, 1972, the national Pastoral Centre was established.[88]

Because of the interest the St Peter's model generated among parish priests in both urban and rural areas, Fr Bex felt obliged to write about the model in detail in a pastoral series that was published in 1976.[89] The report, covering the period 1969 to 1974, documents a 'fairly massive campaign to build small churches with committed communities'.[90] Due to the success of the experiment at St Peter's, the term 'small Christian community' became a catchword in the pastoral endeavours across the country during the seventies and eighties. We will briefly explore how this concept was popularised before it became a nationally approved ecclesiological model.

## The Driefontein National Pastoral Consultation: November, 1972

This consultation was facilitated by the newly founded National Pastoral Centre, established in March 1972 to coordinate and develop a programme of pastoral renewal.[91] The consultation was attended by representatives from dioceses across the country. The representatives, who were all clergy, resolved that the establishment of 'responsible local Christian communities' was one of the pastoral priorities of the Church in Rhodesia. In their view, the local Christian community did not coincide with the traditional parish or former mission structure.[92] This national consultation defined the local Christian community as 'a group of people sharing common territorial area and common community sentiment on grounds of common active belief in Christ'.[93]

The same consultation listed a variety of activities and functions that the local Christian communities were to serve. These ranged from preaching, teaching catechism, organising liturgical services, having Sunday services without a priest to engaging in pastoral services such as visiting and assisting the sick, providing care for the disabled and blind and ministering to the lapsed.[94]

According to the participants at the Driefontein consultation, greater participation of the laity in the local Christian communities was not a mere pragmatic necessity in the face of shortage of priestly vocations. Rather, it was viewed as a theological rediscovery of the right of the laity in the Church.[95] The consultants hoped that giving the laity the sole responsibility for organising the communities, would make them aware of their spiritual and material needs which they could not solve individually. The consultants therefore viewed the local small Christian community as an ecclesiological model that would promote and sustain personal and community growth through inter-personal relationships in Christ.[96]

## The National Seminar and Workshop on the Formation of Basic Christian Communities in Rhodesia: December, 1973

After about a year of digesting recommendations from the Driefontein consultation, a national seminar was organised, at the Gokomere Training Centre, in December 1973. As in the previous consultation, all dioceses were represented and a substantial number of lay people, especially catechists, attended.[97] The theme of the seminar reflected the thinking of the clergy and bishops on the necessity of forming local Christian communities.

The aim of the seminar was:

> to collect information from people involved in the work of building Christian communities in order to get new insights and fresh inspiration, and possibly some measure of cooperation in the future.[98]

Such information was considered very important for consideration by two episcopal institutions. The first was the commission on Catechetics founded in 1971 to co-ordinate national initiatives on catechetics after many Catholic leaders had abondoned teaching Catholic faith in the classroom;[99] the second was the Pastoral centre.

It was at this seminar that the model adopted by St Peter's was given the spotlight. Also of interest at this seminar were pastoral endeavours by the St Anthony's parish of Bulawayo. The St Anthony's Christian communities were already developing local liturgies that were designed to meet the needs of particular communities.[100]

At this seminar, participants were also informed of the rather advanced phase which the diocese of Wankie had attained regarding the building of small Christian communities. At a meeting attended by representatives from Mozambique, Zambia and Rhodesia, and held at Wankie in August, 1972, the Spanish Burgos Fathers manning the rural diocese of Wankie had adopted a resolution to develop small Christian communities.[101] That this meeting came before the Driefontein consultation meant that Wankie diocese had a reasonably long time to popularise the new concept. At this seminar, Wankie's report was the most comprehensive because it already had small Christian communities of three varieties, that is, mass centres, former mission outstations centred around what was formerly a Church primary school, and 'basic' communities which constituted parts of mass centres.[102] Wankie diocese stressed the importance of Christian communities being made aware of the need to be economically self-supporting.[103] This was one of the many elements from the diocese of Wankie that was adopted by the participants at the Gokomere workshop.[104]

In a report given by the representative of Gwelo diocese, a long history of consciousness regarding the importance of the local Christian community had stemmed from an article that Fr Patrick Galvin had published in 1966.[105] Although Gwelo diocese had not translated this consciousness into action, its representative to the seminar also stressed the need for self-support in the Church.

'The local people are still far from providing for ordinary support of their pastor, which has to be subsidized,'[106] the diocesan representative noted. The building of local Christian communities, which the representative regarded as 'dynamic churches', was therefore viewed as a way to increase the financial accountability by the local Church so that it would no longer depend on the churches overseas.[107]

At the conclusion of the seminar held at Gokomere those dioceses which had small Christian communities went away more confident and were prepared to build more. Those dioceses where nothing substantial had been done, like Umtali, were convinced of the necessity for the new model. The small Christian community model was therefore adopted and approved nationally at the end of 1973.

## Conclusion

The period from the mid-1960s to the early 1970s was indeed a testing time for the Catholic Church in Zimbabwe. Challenged by new acclesiological insights from the Second Vatican Council, the local hierarchy was bound to meet opposition when reforms were introduced from the top without due consideration to local preconditions. Early attempts to reinforce the local Church by means of parish councils and lay associations were thus counteracted by active lay members in the Catholic Association.

However as the political atmosphere became increasingly harsher the Church was forced to pursue policies in favour of local Christian communities. The conflict of the Church with the UDI Government over educational policies led the Church to hand over its primary schools to local councils and to develop new means of local evangelism.

From the early 1970s onwards there evolved two strategies that were not necessarily mutually exclusive. One was represented by the Catholic Association in the Salisbury Archdiocese, which linked its concern for local Christian relevance with the task of articulating a political protest against the minority regime of Ian Smith. This venture, though, was refuted by the leadership of the Church, which in this diocese was dominated by the Jesuit order. For them security lay in making a clear demarcation between politics and religion.

The other strategy, which gradually captivated the attention of the Church at a broader inter-diocesan level, contained a more flexible way of running the local parishes by means of establishing small Christian communities. In this way the new community ecclesiology from the Second Vatican Council could be pursued and locally appropriated. The inspiration from the Council also reinforced attempts for more localised orders of worship.

## Notes

1. Decree on the Apostolate of the Laity, No. 10.
2. Randolph R H, *Report to Rome*, p. 98.
3. Fr Pat Galvin, Interview at Pastoral Centre, on 15 June, 1991.
4. Chikuvire, E, Interview at Chivhu, on 14 August 1991.
5. Dachs, A J and W Rea, *The Catholic Church and Zimbabwe (1879-1979)*, p. 168.
6. *Ibid.*
7. *Ibid.*
8. Appendix to Minutes of the RCBC meeting held from 16-20 February, 1970. In File A2/MB 70 of the General Secretariat Archives.
9. *Catholic Teachers' Newsletter*, No. 84, March, 1971, p.1. In Archdiocese Archives.
10. *Ibid.*
11. *Ibid.*
12. *Ibid.*
13. *Ibid.*
14. *Ibid.*, p.2
15. *Ibid.*
16. *Ibid.*
17. RCBC Newsletter, No.21, April, 1970, p.9.
18. *Catholic Directory of Rhodesia*, 1970, Appendix 1.
19. Randolph, *op.cit.*, p. 76.
20. *Ibid.*
21. *Catholic Directory of Rhodesia*, cf. note 18.
22. RCBC Meeting held from 16 to 20 February, 1970. Cf. report by Bishop Haene, p.2. In General Secretariat Archives.
23. Rev T Jakata, Interview at Gokomere Training Centre on 18 February, 1990.
24. *Ibid.*
25. RCBC Meeting, Cf. note 22, p.3.
26. *Ibid.*
27. Supra, pp. 70 - 71.
28. Daniels, G M, *Drums of War*, p. 119.
29. Hastings, A, *Church and Mission in Modern Africa*, p. 87.
30. National Catechetical Committee Report, June, 1972, p. 2. In General Secretariat Archives.

31. Randolph, *op.cit.*, p. 45.
32. RCBC Meeting with CMRS on 9 November, 1970, p.8. In General Secretariat Archives.
33. *Ibid.*
34. *Ibid.*
35. Rev Hector Farrina, Interview at Harare on 16 July, 1992.
36. Fr T Jakata, Interview at Gokomere Training Centre on 25 September, 1991.
37. Bishop Markall's letter to Mission Superiors, 4 July 1970. Cf. BM file at the General Secretariat.
38. *Ad. Clerum*, 28 May, 1970. In Harare diocese Archives.
39. Minutes of the meeting between Archbishop Markall and mission Superiors held on 28th May, 1970, pp. 1 - 2. In Harare diocese Archives.
40. McLoughlin, T O was to lead these courses. Cf, Minutes of the Meeting convened by Archbishop Markall referred to in note 39.
41. *Lumen Gentium*, No. 40.
42. Archdiocese report of the Regional CA of 24 February, 1970, p.2. In Harare diocese Archives.
43. Archbishop Markall had worked with the CA movement since 1955 as Spiritual Advisor of the Salisbury region. He is the one who wrote to Mission Superiors.
44. CA report of the Congress held at St Paul's Musami from 22nd to 24th August, 1969, p.4. See also minutes of the Territorial Council of the CA held on 11th December, 1969, p.1. In the Harare diocese Archives.
45. Zawaira T, Interview at Masvingo on 19 May 1991.
46. Minutes of *Ad. hoc.* Committee Meeting of the C.A. Territorial Council held on 16 December, 1971, p.2. In Harare diocese Archives.
47. *Ibid.*, p.5.
48. *Ibid.*
49. Messers, T Zawaira, T Mutyambizi and E Muchenje constituted the *Ad hoc.* Committee. Interview with T. Zawaira on 19 May, 1991.
50. *Ibid.*
51. *Ibid.*
52. *Ibid.*
53. *Ibid.*
54. Archbishop Markall's letter to the territorial Council Secretary of the CA, Mukonyora B., 11 June, 1972. In Harare diocese Archives.
55. Minutes of the meeting of the CA representatives to the Regional Council with Archbishop Markall and episcopal vicars of Marandellas and Sinoia.

Chapter 4 — The 'Local Church' and Local Political Mobilisation    61

Held on 13 September, 1972, p.2. In Harare diocese Archives.
56. Ibid.
57. 46th Meeting of the CA in the Archdiocese of Salisbury, held on 22 December, 1972, p.2. Harare diocese Archives.
58. Ibid.
59. Ibid.
60. Meeting of the CA Territorial Council held at Silveira House on 11 March, 1973, p.1. in Harare diocese Archives.
61. Ibid.
62. Meeting of the CA Territorial Council held at Silveira House on 11 March, 1973, p.1. in Harare diocese Archives.
63. Letter from Spritual Adviser to Chairman of the CA, 24 September 197. In Harare diocese Archives.
64. Fr M Hannan in a letter complaining to Archibishop Markall, 20 August, 1974. In Harare diocese Archives.
65. CA Regional Secretary, Mr Samakomva then wrote a letter to bishop P Chakaipa on 4th October, 1973. In Harare diocese Archives.
66. Ibid.
67. Fr M Hannan, op.cit.
68. Nyatsanza, W, op.cit., p19.
69. Sr Martin, Interview at Highfields, on May 5 1990.
70. Fr McEnhill, Interview at St. Peter's, Mbare on 7 May, 1990.
71. Messrs Moffat, Dunduru and Chifamba, Interview at St Peter's New Church, on 1 May, 1990.
72. Ibid.
73. Chifamba, Interview on 1 May, 1990.
74. Ibid.
75. Bex A., St Peter's Harare, p.24.
76. Ibid.
77. Ibid.
78. Ibid.
79. Ibid.
80. Ibid.
81. Vhuta, Interview at St Peter's New Church, on 16 February, 1992.
82. Ibid.
83. Bex, op.cit., p. 24.
84. Ibid.

85. *Ibid.*
86. *Ibid.*
87. Fr R H Randolph, Interview at Prestage House, on 04 September, 1988.
88. Randolph, R H, *Report to Rome*, p. 58.
89. Bex, *St Peter's Harare*, 1976.
90. *Ibid.*, p. 27
91. Randolph, *Report to Rome*, p.58.
92. Minutes of the National Consultation held at Driefontein (1972). In General Secretariat Archives.
93. *Ibid.*, p. 1.
94. *Ibid.*, p.2.
95. *Ibid.*
96. *Ibid.*
97. *Ibid.* (These were 9 catechists and 21 priests).
98. Letter of Invitation, dated 27 September, 1973, p.1. In the Lay Aposotlate File in the Harare diocese Archives.
99. Randolph R H, *Report to Rome*, p. 18.
100. Fr A Alapont of St Antony's parish, Bulawayo gave a talk at the Seminar and Workshop. Cf. Minutes, p.4 in the Lay Apostolate file in Harare diocese Archives.
101. RCBC Newsletter, No. 38, September, 1973, p.3.
102. Minutes of the Workshop and Seminar held at Gokomere, p.5. cf. note 98.
103. *Ibid.*
104. *Ibid.*
105. Pat Galvin, 'The formation of the Christian Community in Rural Areas.', In *Guti*, No.14, 1966, pp.41-68.
106. Minutes of the Seminar and Workshop held at Gokomere, p. 11. (Harare Archdiocese Archives).
107. *Ibid.*, p. 13.

# PART II

# THE 'LOCAL CHURCH' AND SOCIAL JUSTICE

## Chapter 5

# New Institutional Means to Pursue Old Priorities in the 'Local Church'

## Introduction

The second dimension of how the new emphases from Vatican II were appropriated and implemented in Zimbabwe concerns the involvement of the local church in justice and peace issues. More evidently than the issues discussed in Part I, this issue has captivated the attention of scholars both from Zimbabwe and from the broader academic community world-wide. And rightly so because the activities of the Catholic Commission for Justice and Peace (CCJP) do represent a courageous ministry of service for the sake of the oppressed people of Zimbabwe.

We will not, in this study, repeat the works of Diana Auret, Sr J. McLaughlin and Ian Linden, which we recognise as major inspiration for this work. Instead we will test how the new insights from the Second Vatican Council regarding justice and peace were interpreted within the local context and concerns within Zimbabwe. Just as the new organisational means for the rallying of Catholic participation in the 'local Church' ran counter to previous Catholic lay movements more notably the Catholic Association, we will also in this case register — at least in the initial phase — a remarkable lack of communication with that Association which in the early 1970s mobilised local Catholic opposition against international ventures to perpetuate the racialist minority regime. As things moved on, however, the ministry of the Commission for justice and peace during the latter part of the 1970s provided openings for new and cordial interaction between the liberation movements and the Church. This interaction had significant repercussions on the Church's position in independent Zimbabwe.

As we have done in Part I we will also introduce Part II with a brief summary of the new insights that the Catholic Church in Zimbabwe, after the Second Vatican Council, had to make and shape its own ministry accordingly. In this regard we have to go beyond ecclesial structural concerns in the strict sense, and briefly refer to the new Catholic social ethics that evolved in the course of, and after, the Council. What is at stake here, thus, is to determine the way or ways in which the 'local Church' became involved in the struggle for social justice.

## A new concern for justice and peace

Quite early on the Rhodesian Catholic Bishops' Conference recognised the importance of the Second Vatican Council documents like *Gaudium et Spes* (1965) and post-conciliar encyclicals like *Populorum Progressio* (1967) and *Octogesima Adveniens* (1971). Firstly the document *Gaudium et Spes* considers it incumbent upon the Church to scrutinise the signs of the times and to interpret them in the light of the gospel.[1] It emphasises the dignity of the human person arguing that the human being is the centre and crown of all things on earth.

Humanisation of the world, the document argues, comes about 'when each person devotes himself to the cause of peace with renewed vigour'.[2] However, *Gaudium et Spes* summons all Christians not to make humanisation a good in itself but to transcend it, with all men under the help of 'Christ the author of life', through cooperation, in securing among themselves a peace based on justice and love and in setting up the instruments of peace.

According to this document:

> Peace is not merely the absence of war; nor can it be reduced solely to the remittance of a balance of power between enemies; nor is brought about by dictatorship. Instead, it is rightly and appropriately called an 'enterprise of justice'. (Is. 32:7)[3]

*Gaudium et Spes* also argues that peace is obtained when personal well-being is safeguarded and people freely and trustingly share with one another the riches of their inner spirits and their talents.

The first post-conciliar document that needs to be highlighted is *Populorum Progressio*, which Pope Paul VI delivered on 26 March 1967. This document is significant because of its radical slant in treating peace and justice as integral components in development.

It corrects the misconception that development means merely economic growth. On the contrary, the document argues for integral development, that is, the promotion of 'the good of the whole man'.[4] It also corrects the wrong impression often made by people in equating a mere absence of war to peace:

> No, peace is something that is built up day after day, in the pursuit of an order intended by God, which implies a more perfect form of justice among men.[5]

Furthermore, *Populorum Progressio* points at structural inequalities among peoples as a danger to peace. It calls upon communities to wage war on misery and to struggle against injustice as a way of promoting, along with other improved conditions, the human spiritual progress of all men, and therefore the common good of humanity.[6]

Thirdly, *Octogesima Adveniens* was delivered on 14 May 1971 at the 80th anniversary of the encyclical *Rerum Novarum* from 1891. This document highlighted the need for the Christian communities to analyse objectively the situation proper to their own country, in order:

> to shed on it the light of the Gospel's words and to draw principles of reflection, norms of judgement and directives for action from the social teachings of the Church.[7]

The Pope emphasised the importance of equality for all members of humanity:

> The members of mankind share the same basic rights and duties, as well as the same supernatural destiny. Within a country which belongs to each one, all should be equal before the law, find equal admittance to economic, cultural, civic and social life and benefit from a fair sharing of the nation's riches.[8]

It was *Octogesima Adveniens* that specifically identified people or sectors of society that in the Church's view were 'victims of situations of injustice'. Among these it placed, those who are discriminated against, in law or in fact, on account of their race, origin colour, culture, sex or religion.[9]

However, the more immediate inspiration for the formation of the Justice and Peace Commission in Rhodesia came from the Synod of Bishops held in Rome from September to December 1971. One of the two topics discussed at this assembly of Bishops was 'Justice in the World'.[10] Without necessarily summarising the conclusions and recommendations of the 1971 synod, it is important to refer to the Pope's announcement to the Church regarding the Day of Peace for 1 January 1972. This announcement had serious implications for the Roman Catholic Church in Rhodesia in terms of developing a programme for peace and justice.

## The call for a day of peace, 1972

In June, 1971, about three months before the Synod of Bishops, Pope Paul VI announced the theme for the day of peace for 1972. He chose a theme that was in line with, and that would prepare the Church for, the Synod of Bishops. 'If you want peace, work for justice', was the challenge to the Church and to the world. Pope Paul called upon the whole Church to reflect on this theme in order for the coming celebration on 1 January, 1972 to be meaningful.

The theme, the Pope noted, had focal relevance to the seventies:

> Its point of departure is a definite lived reality; the countless injustices throughout the world. It meets the expectations of the men and women of today; the discovery of evil and the sin of the world arouses their indignation and their desire to act or to fight against it.[11]

The theme chosen for this day of peace was meant to ensure that the work of the Synod of Bishops would be followed up, and implemented in a practical way at the level of local churches. In the light of the forthcoming Synod and day of peace, the Pope called upon episcopal conferences to draw up programmes of educating Catholics on the need for peace and justice.[12] This call was supported by the colourful Synod of Bishops, when they met for the first time in November 1971.

## The document *Evangelii Nuntiandi*

When the Synod of Bishops, which was convened in Rome in November 1971, was coming to an end, declarations were agreed upon concerning the two topics that had been under discussion. Our concern here is with the declarations that pertain to peace and justice. The Bishops noted that wherever citizens are capable of influencing their own destiny through active participation in community and national affairs, they are bound to carry their Christianity fully into public life. This means that, in the human situation, there must be involvement of all Christians, and an involvement in all situations. This is a truly active and meaningful expression of brotherly love. This love implies an absolute demand for justice, namely recognition of the dignity and rights of our neighbour.[13]

The Bishops specifically called upon the Church to preach universal brotherhood, to highlight the need for justice, and to denounce concrete situations of injustice 'when the fundamental rights and salvation of man require it'.[14] Furthermore the Synod underscored the need for local churches to impart within their members a continuing education for justice. In essence this type of education was viewed as practical and result of 'action, participation vital contact with the reality of justice.'[15] The goal of education for justice was to help oppressed people to be no longer the object of manipulation by communications media or political forces. It would instead enable them to take in hand their destinies and bring about communities that are truly human.[16]

According to Bishop Donal Lamont, who represented the Rhodesia Catholic Bishops' Conference at the Synod, a 'new course' was being charted for the Church. Throughout the Synod of Bishops, the Church had demonstrated a 'new concern with being involved in a practical way by promoting the freedom of the whole man and of every man, and of recognizing this as an integral part of its mission'.[17]

Both the Pope's address focusing on the day of peace and the Synod of Bishops provide some ambit within which to evaluate the work on the Justice and Peace Commission in Rhodesia. As we will see shortly, Bishop Lamont had not only contributed to the Synod but had learnt a lot out of it. When he returned to his diocese he was ready for action.

## Notes

1. *Gaudium et Spes*, No.4.
2. *Ibid.*, No. 77.
3. *Ibid.*, No.78.
4. *Populorum Progressio*, No.14.
5. *Ibid.*, No.76.
6. *Ibid.*
7. *Octogesima Adveniens*, No.4.
8. *Ibid.*, No. 17.
9. *Ibid.*, No.16.
10. RCBC Newsletter, No. 15, May, 1972, p.4.
11. RCBC Newsletter, No. 12, February, 1972, p.30.
12. *Ibid.*
13. 'Justice in the world, Synod of Bishops, Nov. 30, 1971', in P Mainelli, (compiler) *Official Catholic Teachings: Social Justice*, p. 293.
14. *Ibid.*
15. *Ibid.*, p. 296
16. *Ibid.*
17. RCBC Newsletter, No. 18, August, 1972, p.4.

Chapter 6

# A New Means of Catholic Service: The Justice and Peace Commission (1972–80)

## Introduction

As already implied above it was the Justice and Peace Commission that from 1972 became the primary instrument of the Catholic Church in Zimbabwe in the implementation of the new and more radical social ethics articulated by the Second Vatican Council. The aim of this chapter is to investigate the extent to which the Justice and Peace Commission of the Roman Catholic Church in Rhodesia, from the time of inception in 1972 up to independence in 1980, functioned as an agent for change within the Church and the nation at large. In our historical examination of the Justice and Peace commission we will focus on the objectives of its formation, the composition and structure of the organisation, its education and decentralisation programmes, and its impact on the struggle for liberation. Last, but not least, we examine how the Commission related to its local base, that is, the 'local Church'.

## Formative years and relations to the Catholic Association (1972–74)

### A new initiative

It was out of the calls from the Pope and the preparatory reflections on the forthcoming Synod of Bishops that the idea to form a Justice and Peace Commission was first raised. This was at a RCBC plenary session in July 1971. The participants at this meeting agreed that consultations aimed at setting up a Justice and Peace Commission should begin at all levels of the Church in Rhodesia.[1] Consultative meetings began in August, 1971, at national, diocesan, and parish council levels. These meetings considered how the local church could share in the practical implementation of the social teachings of the Church, particularly in the fields of justice, peace, and development in accordance with the stated desire of Pope Paul VI.[2]

The consultations culminated in a meeting held on 20 November 1971, at Chishawasha (Silveira House), chaired by Bishop A Haene. Twenty-eight people from all dioceses attended this meeting. They included the Chairman of the National Council of the Laity, executive members of the conference of major Religious Superiors (men and women of the Salisbury Archdiocese), Pastoral Council and episcopal Theological Commission together with the heads of several religious orders and lay representatives, both black and white.[3] The representative of different church bodies brought with them the results 'written and oral, of consultations which had taken place in recent weeks.'[4]

The Chishawasha meeting formulated and forwarded the recommendations to the Bishops' Conference calling for the immediate formation of a national Commission for Justice and Peace.[5] In its declaration the meeting noted:

> Love of God and love of man cannot be divided. The Christian Gospel has to be put into practice here and now, without fear or favour. This programme will be the special concern of the National Commission for Justice and Peace.[6]

At the conclusion of its deliberations the meeting decided to set up an interim committee of the Justice and Peace Commission. This committee was tasked with the responsibility to initiate a programme of action and to draw up a draft constitution for the substantive Justice and Peace Commission. This committee was also tasked with drawing up the terms of reference for the substantive Commission in its relations to the RCBC and its financial support.[7] According to Bishop Haene, the Interim Committee was established 'to all intents and purposes as the Commission for the time being'. [8]

It is not clear what were the criteria for electing the members of the Interim Committee. However, this interim body found itself consisting of four members from Salisbury archdiocese and three from Gwelo diocese.[9] All the members of this Committee were white in spite of the presence of nine black representatives at the Chishawasha meeting.[10]

At the bishops' plenary meeting in Bulawayo held two months after the establishment of the Interim Committee a commitment was made to work towards the improvement of channels of communication between the RCBC and grassroots levels of the Church.[11] The commitment, however, fell short of any practical suggestions. But what is important to note here is that there was, within the Bishops' Conference, an awareness that decisions being taken at national levels of the Church were not getting across to the majority of Catholics in the country.

Ironically, while the Bishops were aware of the dichotomy between national and grassroot levels, at the same meeting, they approved the membership of the substantive Justice and Peace Commission, proposed by the national Interim Committee. They also approved the Draft Constitution of the Justice and Peace Commission which was prepared by the Interim Committee. No questions were raised whether the Interim Committee had carried out consultations in the dioceses and parishes before coming up with a draft constitution and suggestions of possible members of the executive of the Commission.[12] There was complete trust in the objectivity of this Interim Committee.

On 2 March 1972 the substantive Justice and Peace Commission, with a constitution approved for three years, was inaugurated. Its objectives were:

(i) to form peoples' consciences; to influence the education and shaping of public opinion in accordance with the Gospel and the teaching of the Church on matters of justice and peace;

(ii) to obtain and disseminate factual and objective information concerning the social organisation of people in Rhodesia; to examine the nature and effect of the controls exercised on the same people and make recommendations as to how social structures and controls can be improved; and

(iii) to investigate allegations of injustices which it considers merit attention, and to publish its findings and take any corrective action in its power.[13]

Although the Commission was an organ of, and responsible to, the RCBC it enjoyed a certain amount of autonomy. The Commission operated differently from, for instance, the liturgical, catechetical or theology commissions. The Justice and Peace Commission would act on the basis of decisions made by its executive committee in consultation with its president who was a bishop. The president provided the liaison between the Commission and the Conference, and decided what matters ought to be referred to the Conference and what matters the Commission should act on its own initiative.[14]

The opinion of the Justice and Peace Commission did not have to be viewed as the official position of the Bishops' Conference.[15] The Commission functioned on the basis of sub-committees that dealt with research, legal, educational, public relations and financial issues. These sub-committees could co-opt members from outside the Commission and the Catholic Church.[16]

Unlike the Interim Committee which was all white in composition, the constituted Commission was conveniently multi-racial. However, the Commission showed insignificant signs of being a model of multiracialism. Out of a total of twenty one members making up the national Commission only six were black. The top executive, chaired by Mr A.J.P.Graham, remained all white. Surprisingly too there was no black diocesan representative.[17]

Without belabouring the point let me hasten to highlight the national statistics of the Catholic Church by the end of 1971.[18]

| Diocese | Catholic Population | |
|---|---|---|
| | African | Non-African |
| Salisbury | 176 853 | 17 251 |
| Gwelo | 154 369 | 4 320 |
| Bulawayo | 51 738 | 10 890 |
| Umtali | 65 445 | 1 184 |
| Wankie | 22 326 | 501 |
| Total | 470 731 | 34 146 |

The explanation behind this racial imbalance in the composition of the Commission appears to have been contained in the system of appointment adopted by Bishop Haene and supported by the RCBC. As we have noted before, the executive and members of the Commission were nominated by the Interim Committee. The Bishops' conference subsequently appointed the members 'on the basis of the positive contribution they [could] make'.[19] Evidently, that basis remained highly subjective. What was clear in the system of appointment put in place was that white elites saw themselves as the people with the right and duty to pick Africans of their liking.

The Bishop's Conference, and indeed, the new Commission completely overlooked the political potential of the Catholic Association which had just completed its mobilisation against the Home-Smith settlement proposals, and, of course, for that reason, was accused of meddling in politics by the hierarchy. This lack of communication between the hierarchy and the Catholic Association was a clear sign that the church was not yet a church of the People — the whole People of God, consisting of both black and white.

Clearly, as Bishop Lamont was later to observe in early 1973, there was something faulty with the composition of the Justice and Peace Commission and perhaps the constitution itself. Among the reasons he raised was that 'the full opinion of the African people [was] not properly represented . . .'[20] Lamont questioned the predominance of whites in the commission. He argued, and rightly so, that:

> While not disputing the competence of the European members and their qualifications, I do not know of anyone of them who has special competence in social ethics.[21]

In August, 1974, when Bishop Haene completed his term of presidency of the Justice and Peace Commission, Lamont was elected to take over. This resulted in Mr A J Graham's resignation as Chairman and member of the Commission.[22] In line with Lamont's thinking Sylvester Maruza, a black lawyer was elected the commission's chairman.[23] Maruza's election to chairmanship was symbolic of the commission's change of perspective regarding the future of the country.

At the time that Maruza got to the helm of the Commission, the war of liberation was escalating. For the commission to earn credibility among the majority of Africans who were embroiled in the war for independence it was important to have a black chairman even if for window-dressing purposes. However, having a fiery president of the likes of Bishop Lamont made the ideological shift towards oppressed and segregated African people more concrete.

Looking back at the first two years of the Justice and Peace Commission, there is little evidence that its establishment was 'a turning point for the Rhodesian Church' as Ian Linden thinks.[24] The meeting at Chishawasha of 17 November 1971, which set up the Interim Committee was far from being what he calls 'the first structural commitment to social justice made by the hierarchy'.[25] Such commitment is what Lamont was questioning when he described the Commission and its constitution as 'faulty'.[26] Indeed Linden concedes that the executive that was in power from March 1972 to August 1974 represented what he aptly calls 'the benign face of the white power block'.[27]

If the setting up of the Justice and Peace Commission was an exercise of public relations by the Church in a situation of political change, surely this may be interpreted as nothing short of insulting the intelligence of the African people of Rhodesia. What the hierarchy had done was simply to assist a white liberal elite within Rhodesia to direct and dominate the political discourse in the country masquerading as champions for justice and the oppressed.

It is our contention that had not the war of liberation (which the Church always viewed as violence) not been waged in earnest since December 1972, the Catholic Church in Rhodesia would have continued with its unbridled paternalism towards the African people. Apparently, the type of paternalism that ran deep in the Church coincided with that practised by colonial governments.

An example from a missionary priest and lecturer at the then University College of Rhodesia confirms the existence of paternalism at that time. On a visit to Rome in November 1972 (a month before the war resumed in earnest) Father W Francis Rea, SJ, was invited to interview on Vatican Radio

(International Fides Service). When asked to comment on the political future in Rhodesia, he asserted:

> If power were to be transferred to the Africans in the immediate future, it would be a complete disaster, more so than in countries to the north, because Rhodesia has a more complicated economy. On the other hand, to refuse all political power to the African majority is against papal teaching and also unrealistic, since owing to the very high African birth-rate and low European one, Africans are bound to rule the country in the end. So what the Church tries to do is to teach the Africans that they must not rush things too much and at the same time condemn separate development and teach Europeans that they must prepare themselves to see the African in time to get political power.[28]

No doubt Fr Rea was not able to recognise the significance of the Catholic Association.

## Selling the idea of peace and justice to the people

### Sermon/discussion outlines

In December 1971 the Bishops Conference requested the members of the Interim Committee to initiate an educational campaign on peace and justice. The Committee was asked to run Sermon/Discussion outlines campaign based on the Pope's theme for the World Day of Peace and other social teachings of the Church.[29]

A theological sub-committee created out of the purely white Interim Committee was therefore given the responsibility of designing monthly topics to run for a whole year. The pamphlets, to be distributed to all dioceses, were written in English, Shona and Ndebele. The local Ordinary was viewed as a crucial figure in the distribution of these pamphlets to the parishes.[30]

Once the bishop had distributed the pamphlets to parishes it was expected that the parish priest would study the monthly sermon outline in order to ensure that each sermon he preached had some bearing on justice and peace. The parish priest was also expected to facilitate and animate discussion among his parishioners along the lines suggested by the Commission's outlines.[31]

### The impact of the justice education campaign

As a way of assessing the impact that the Sermon/discussion outlines had on Catholic members, the Justice and Peace Commission launched an evaluation exercise in April 1972. This was first five months after the outlines had been issued. The Commission asked each of the five local bishops for responses to the following three questions:

(i) How many of your clergy have preached on the topics?
(ii) Did the clergy find them useful?
(iii) Did the laity find them useful in each of the three languages?[32]

This evaluation was crucial for the Commission because it would shed some light on the interest it had so far generated on issues of justice and peace among local Catholics.

Diocesan returns revealed, however, that little interest had been generated among the lay Catholics of Salisbury, Bulawayo, Umtali and Wankie dioceses. It was only in Gwelo diocese where the campaign had been successful though 'among community leaders only, rather than whole congregations'.[33] According to the report from Gwelo diocese the Shona version of the Discussion outline was 'often eagerly awaited' by community leaders of many parishes.[34]

In the dioceses of Wankie, Bulawayo and Salisbury some European laymen had, by the time of the evaluation exercise, left the Church in anger and disappointment with the bishops whom they saw as being either 'too much biased in favour of Africans' or 'out of touch with the Europeans'.[35] Most of the white Catholics had not given heed to the sermons or discussions because already in the early 1970s they 'suspected' anything by the bishops as 'interfering in politics'.[36] Many did not realise that the Church's social teaching springs from the Gospel. Others just felt that the bishops were trying to force 'a line of conduct . . . on them'.[37]

According to Bishop I Prieto of Wankie, the role of the priests was crucial in this campaign. The success or failure of the programme was to depend on them.[38] Some preached along the lines of the Outlines only in the early months of the campaign. Others did not preach but 'handed the leaflets to the people, African and European, without much, if any, discussion'.[39] The priests of Salisbury diocese appeared to be most unfavourable to the Sermon/discussion outlines.

Of the 150 priests asked to respond to the questionnaires only 15 per cent did. The lack of interest in the Sermon/discussion outlines on the part of the clergy in the cities was particularly noticeable.[40] However, two African parishes in Salisbury had got motivated by their priests. Not least St Peter's in Mbare had registered an average attendance of seventy-five people at discussion gatherings. [41]

## Implications of the evaluation exercise in terms of future operations of the commission

For any development programme to succeed, it is important to identify and consult the key players who are supposed to implement it. In the case of the Justice and Peace campaign carried out in 1972, the Commission relied on the bishops as the key players. The bishops on their part appear not to have adequately consulted the parish priests, that is, the players with direct contact with the local Catholics. At the same time the bishops did not consult the diocesan pastoral councils or diocesan lay associations. Such wide consultation could have broadened the base of the players.

Furthermore, the bishops mainly directed their attention to the priests. In the process they showed a lack of confidence in the new lay structures that they had set in motion in the Church since 1969. To complicate matters, most of the bishops simply commended the Sermons/discussion outlines to the majority of the clergy in a written *Ad Clerum*. This armchair style of running the campaign did not amuse many priests, especially in Salisbury archdiocese, where priests argued that they were not consulted. Twenty-five per cent of the priests who responded to the questionnaire 'complained that nothing had been done to 'sell' the idea to the clergy, and resented the appearance of it having been imposed from above without consultation'.[42]

The approach adopted by the Bishop A Haene of Gwelo was, however, more personal compared with that of his colleagues. He introduced the programme to the priests and discussed it at two meetings, 'one for all the priests of the English speaking congregations,[43] and one for the majority of priests in Shona speaking congregations'. Because of the positive impact of this personal approach, the priests at deanery level discussed further ways and means of effectively reaching out to their parishioners.[44]

A sense of local identification with the programme appears to have been created in the priests in Gwelo diocese. Because the priests felt that they were part of the decision making body, they freely involved educated lay leaders, catechists, teachers, and others to introduce the subject after having studied the monthly leaflet.[45] In some cases, the monthly copies were discussed 'at the monthly meeting of community leaders who in turn were expected to deal with the topic in their communities'.[46]

Apart from the parish, there were other institutions within the Church which had to be catered for. These included secondary schools, teacher training colleges and training colleges for nurses. At an African Secondary School, the leaflets were first discussed at a staff meeting, then distributed among the students and finally discussed during the religious instruction period.

Gwelo diocese thus appears to have used a variety of structures and players in order to publicise the campaign. It was not surprising therefore that there came positive results from this diocese from the following observation, 'A great number of African communities hold regular meetings on the topic of the month and they are well-attended.'[48]

There could, of course, be other reasons to explain the failure of the campaign in other dioceses and the success in Gwelo diocese. However, in my opinion, the way responsibility was passed on from the superior to the subordinate level significantly contributed to the attitude those at the subordinate level had towards change.

Nevertheless the Sermon/discussion outlines were generally a failure. According to the responses from the dioceses, Church members shared the sentiment that the setting up of the Justice and Peace Commission and the Sermon/discussion campaign, was long overdue and that the Church had failed in its prophetic calling. A response by one layman from the Archdiocese of Salisbury summarised this thinking thus:

> The exercise is five years too late: the Church in Rhodesia reads the signs of times when it is too late, and then interprets them to the advantage of the Church, which is always right, though often proved wrong.[49]

This assessment was confirmed even by some of the European laity who saw the campaign as 'too late for meaningful dialogue between Europeans and Africans' and who also considered the Church to have 'been too passive in the past to claim a real appreciation now of the seriousness of the situation without previous preparation'.[50] T O McLoughlin therefore makes an appropriate observation when he noted:

> The point is that the reaction of both Africans and Europeans to their Bishops' teaching will continue to be determined by political hopes and fears until that teaching has an adequate point of appeal in the faith and conscience of the people.[51]

While for the large sections of laity the campaign came too late, for many of the priests, it came too early. Most of them were not ready to preach the new 'gospel'. Even those who preached along the lines suggested in the outlines 'found it difficult to devote one sermon every month on such a topic and they [had] the feeling that they [had] exhausted the subject after one or two sermons'.[52]

This was a clear demonstration of the priests' lack of imagination in their pastoral commitment. Not only that but also that the priests were out of touch with their African congregations. Evidently, they were ideologically ill-prepared to grapple with the issues pertaining to a just order where both black and white could live in peace and harmony. Because of their failure to draw on the needs and aspirations of the African people, these priests were little different from those who refused to preach about justice in order 'to avoid trouble'.[53]

Prophecy thus was sacrificed at the altar of 'security'. The great majority of the missionary priests, who were still more than 80 per cent of the priesthood in the Church in Rhodesia, saw their interests being catered for by the colonial hegemony. In their thinking, the time had not yet come for the Church to make a prophetic call against the injustices and evils plaguing the Rhodesian Society, or rather they could not see these injustices.

Although the Sermon/discussion outlines were on the whole unsuccessful, there were some positive developments registered in the dioceses of Bulawayo, Gwelo and Umtali in late 1972. Diocesan committees of the Justice and Peace were founded in these dioceses. The committees in Bulawayo and Gwelo embarked on research programmes to investigate wage structures for African workers. The Bulawayo committee also carried out investigations on Christian burial ceremonies among the citizens of Bulawayo city.[54]

Meanwhile the Umtali diocese committee focused attention on providing relief to, and sensitising the nation on, the plight of the Tangwena children who had been turned into victims as a result of the Land Tenure Act.[55] The Committee also carried out research on the cost of living in Sakubva suburb.[56] This promised real advances in the coming period.

## The JPC in the midst of war (1973–78)

### The war of liberation

By the end of December 1972, the liberation war intensified from the North-eastern front. The National Commission for Justice and Peace therefore was forced to direct its efforts towards reporting the plight of the African people in war-stricken parts of the country. The new situation meant that less and less effort could be placed on education programmes for peace and justice. A crisis seemed to have overtaken the Church's plans. The few discussion groups that had sprouted were now forced to attend to new interactions with the freedom fighters. There was also fear by the priests that the discussion groups were invariably becoming more and more 'political' in a more and more partisan way. The natural response for the parish was priests to discourage such trends.[57] Not surprisingly, the proposed National Symposium, which was to be held at the end of 1973, fell through.[58]

From 1973 up to 1977, the Justice and Peace Commission was forced by circumstances to operate on an *ad hoc* and reactive basis as its operations became associated more and more with collating and publicising individual cases of atrocities, human rights violations, and cases of repression perpetrated by the military and para-military arms of the Rhodesian State.[59]

## *New priorities for JPC*

As the war raged on, 1974 brought about a new resolve in the commission as it faced greater hostility from the Government. In March, 1974, it produced a dossier of brutalities allegedly committed by the Rhodesian Security Forces and shared its contents with the Government. The Commission called on the Government to set up a commission of enquiry to be chaired by 'a man of calibre and qualification like Sir Robert Tredgold'[60] Because of inaction by the Government the Commission took recourse through its attorneys to the High Court.[61]

The challenge of the Government at law forced the latter to pass '*The Indemnity and Compensation Act* (1975)', a piece of legislation which effectively prevented any other security-related cases from being heard and judged in any court of the land. The Act also protected the security forces and the Minister of Defence from prosecution.[62] However, this did not silence the Church.

Testifying before a United Nations Committee on Rhodesia, during his visit to the United States of America in May 1974, Bishop Donal Lamont said that the black people in the country were living under a reign of terror comparable to Nazi Germany.[63] This was Lamont's first public comment on this repressive Act. From then on he never relented in his attacks on the racist Rhodesian government. In August, 1974, Lamont was to head the Justice and Peace Commission up to February 1977, when he was deported. He is the man who with Sylvester Maruza and Etherton Mupisaunga as chairman, consolidated the work of the Commission in its new dispensation.

From 1975 the Commission decided openly to publicise the plight of the people which they had been able to investigate. The first such publication was *Man in the Middle* (1975) which was published in London by the Catholic International Institute for Race Relations (CIIR). Summaries of this document appeared in both the *London Times* and the *Irish Times* as well as in several European and Southern African Dailies.[64] *Man in the Middle* highlighted the torture of civilians suspected by the security forces to have had contact or collaboration with freedom fighters, whom the Rhodesian government labelled 'terrorists'. The document also exposed the forced eviction and resettlement of people from their homes into 'protected villages'. These villages were established by the government as an attempt to cut off links between the guerrillas and the people.[65]

In October 1976 the Justice and Peace Commission produced another loaded dossier entitled *Civil War in Rhodesia*. The publication of this document coincided with the sentence of Bishop Lamont at the Umtali High Court. As soon as it was out the Rhodesian government banned it.

*Civil war in Rhodesia* represents a radicalisation of the position of the Justice and Peace Commission. It categorically denied that guerrilas were 'terrorists' or represented a communist force as invaders from outside the country. Rather it argued that guerrillas were:

> citizens of the country ... fighting for the right of self-determination for their fellow blacks and for a share in the wealth which would enable them to live their lives in conditions of basic physical health and social decency.[66]

The dossier also highlights the suffering of black civilians. It reported intimidation through demonstrations of fire power and shooting of curfew breakers by the Rhodesian forces. Furthermore, it exposed the government's propaganda machinery and practices like displaying dead guerrillas and offering prizes for reporting 'terrorists'. In this dossier, the Justice and Peace Commission stressed what it called the law of love and reconciliation between peoples. But reconciliation alone will not solve 'the country's problems; reconciliation must be accompanied by the desire and will to change.'[67]

It further called upon the perpetrators of injustices to redress the situation as soon as they could. The victims of injustice were likewise called to accept peace and to forgive. This was the only promising alternative for the future prosperity of the country, the Commission argued. Tim Sheehy and Eileen Sudworth view the two dossiers referred to above as a clear example of the Justice and Peace Commission's commitment to take up the gauntlet and to challenge strongly actions of the Rhodesian regime and its officers.[68]

From these two dossiers one sees a definite departure from the official definition and perception of the liberation struggle. The Justice and Peace Commission adopted the perception of the rank and file especially the rural Christians who would not theorise on which side to support but enthusiastically welcomed the guerrillas as their children or brothers and sisters.

In its new and more articulate stage the Justice and Peace Commission found ready support in its Chairman, Bishop Donal Lamont of Umtali diocese. Just about a month before the publication of *Civil War in Rhodesia* he wrote an open letter to the government of Rhodesia. There he affirmed:

> Conscience compels me to state that your administration by its clearly racist and oppressive policies and by its stubborn refusal to change is largely responsible for the injustices which have provoked

the present disorder and it must in that measure be considered guilty of whatever misery or bloodshed follows.[69]

Lamont questioned the grounds on which the Rhodesian government at one time based their claim to rule. 'Such argument no longer has validity. You may rule with the consent of a small and selfish electorate, but you rule without the consent of the nation.'[70]

Radical though Lamont sounded, he fell short of calling on the Christians to join the revolution out of love for fellow men. Lamont was quite clear that when the existing administration is against the majority of the people, it is not legitimate, but a tyranny. But he did not, like Camilo Torres, have the courage to say, 'We Christians can and must fight against tyranny'.[71] Even so Lamont's open letter was an invaluable encouragement to many supporters of the liberation struggle. [72]

In 1977 the foremost international supporter of the JPC, that is, the London-based Catholic Institute of International Relations (CIIR) published *Rhodesia: The Propaganda War* after having been supplied with confidential information from the Commission's 'Fact Papers' by Sr Janice McLaughlin.[73] The dossier dealt with various aspects of the war, such as civilian deaths, rural breakdown, 'protected villages' and government propaganda to isolate the guerrillas. It also carried stories of torture, security legislation, the financial cost of the war, the creation of new war zones and secret hangings.

All in all, the dossiers were meant to bring to light the truth of the war situation and the repression in Rhodesia. Through these publications the Justice and Peace Commission managed to sensitise the international community of the side of the story that the Government media omitted for deliberate political reasons. It was through these publications that the extent of Government repression and 'security forces' harassment of the rural people became widely known.

## The JPC and the internal settlement

### Identifying a new dialogue partner

The failure in 1976 of the Anglo-American sponsored conference at Geneva to come up with a political solution led to talks within Rhodesia between Ian Smith and some of the internal leaders. This resulted in the internal settlement of 3 March 1978, to which Ian Smith, Ndabaningi Sithole, Abel Muzorewa and Jeremiah Chirau were signatories. This agreement was viewed by the Justice and Peace Commission and the Rhodesia Bishops' Conference as an 'unfortunate development' whose ultimate intent was 'to further divide the country and plunge it into a more ravaging civil war'.[74] In this regard the Commission was supported by the CIIR in denouncing the settlement.

As the internal leaders, who now formed the interim government, were bracing themselves for elections in April 1979, the Bishops' Conference and the Commission saw greater need for the Church to mediate between the two belligerents, that is the Internal leaders and the Patriotic Front. After two meetings which the Commission and the Bishops' Conference attended it was agreed that real peace could only come to Rhodesia as a result of a common settlement by both camps or through a violent takeover of the Government by the Patriotic Front. The latter was viewed as a remote possibility and more devasting for the country. It was the former solution that was viewed as capable of bringing about peace and reconciliation.[75]

Throughout the war period the bishops and the Commission had maintained contacts with the Government with a view to encourage them to stop the war. However, no attempts had been made at this official level to contact the ZANU and ZAPU leadership in exile. However at their meeting in June, 1978, the Bishops and the Commission formed a committee comprising Archbishop Patrick Chakaipa, Monsignor Helmut Reckter and Fr Bernard Ndlovu from the Bishops Conference and brother Fidelis Mukonori, Mr Ishmael Muvingi and Mr Michael Auret from the Commission. This Committee was authorised to meet with the ZANU and ZAPU leadership to share views with them on the situation in the country as it affected the people and to plead with them on the possibility of stopping the war.[76]

In order for such a meeting to take place the Committee contacted the Apostolic representative in South Africa, Mozambique, and Zambia to request President Kaunda, then Chairman of the Frontline States, to use his influence on ZANU and ZAPU leaders. Through the active involvement of the Organisation of African Unity it was finally agreed that meetings take place between 13th and 21st August 1978 in Lusaka. The Bishops' Conference and the Committee appointed by the Commission were to meet the ZANU and ZAPU leadership separately.[77]

## Meeting with the ZAPU leaders

The very first meeting between the representatives of the Bishops' Council and the Commission and the ZAPU leadership was also attended by President Kaunda, the Apostolic Nuncio to Zambia, and Archbishop I Milingo of Lusaka. The ZAPU delegation comprised Mr Joshua Nkomo (President), Mr Munodawafa (Chairman), Mr G. Silundika and Mr Gopwe (Foreign Affairs), Mr Stephen Nkomo (Security) and Mr Marembo (Internal Affairs) and few other officials. At the very beginning of this meeting Archbishop

Chakaipa read his delegation's prepared speech which stated the aim of their visit. The speech only contained two very brief points. Firstly his delegation wanted to 'share views' with the Patriotic Front delegation on the situation in Rhodesia as it affected the people and the Church. Secondly, the delegation was in Lusaka to consult the Patriotic Front about 'the role of the Church in the new Zimbabwe'.[78]

The ZAPU President, Joshua Nkomo, in his reply to Bishop Chakaipa's speech, indicated how touched he was by the Church delegation's concern for the people of Zimbabwe. He went on to say that because of their concern for ordinary people, he was himself going to show them the camps for children and young women who had fled Rhodesia and had become a great burden on available resources.

In the next two days, the Church delegation from Rhodesia was taken on guided tours of three camps. The first had about 8 000 boys aged from nine to fifteen years, another had 1000 girls aged between eight and fifteen years, and among them were 113 young mothers aged between thirteen and eighteen years, all with babies.[79]

The guided tour was an eye-opener to the Church delegation from Rhodesia. It provided an opportunity for them to see the misery of the young refugees in the camps as well as the educational programmes and skills-training ventures, such as the dress-making factory run by the young mothers, that ZAPU had put into place. When they were taken to the storerooms that housed the foodstuff and other material resources, they were convinced that the demand outstripped supply by far.[80]

The tour managed to bring the representatives of the Bishops' Conference and the Justice and Peace Commission in direct contact with the refugees. Through talking with them the delegation was made to appreciate their suffering as well as the 'impressive work' that ZAPU was doing for them.[81]

During the tour the Church delegation also got to know about the refugees' thinking regarding the new turn of political affairs in Rhodesia and what they expected of the Church. At the young mothers' camp, the Woman-in-Charge made a long and emotional speech about Christianity and politics:

> To her religious leaders should be religious leaders and leave politics to politicians. She was after Muzorewa particularly and her request to us was to tell Muzorewa that the work of a preacher is to reconcile, not to take sides. He should give up the call because he is bringing it into disrepute.[82]

The Woman-in-Charge was not alone in expressing these sentiments; most of the women spoken to raised the same concern.[83] It was during the tour of the refugee camps that the Church delegation learnt from the ZAPU leader why this party was more inclined towards the then Socialist Block countries like Cuba and the then Union of Soviet Socialist Republic. According to Mr Nkomo, the 'Christian Western countries' had barely supported the struggle and the educational ventures that his party put in place. They also did not support the students that the party wanted to send to Europe or America for tertiary education and skills training, programmes which the party promoted as a way of preparing for the new Zimbabwe. While the socialist countries offered between two hundred and three hundred scholarships each year, the Western countries offered an average of three per year.[84]

After the tour of the refugee camps, a more formal meeting between the ZAPU and the Church representatives took place. Archbishop Chakaipa impressed upon the ZAPU leaders the enormous suffering the people of Rhodesia were subjected to as a result of ' a war situation escalating over the past seven years'.[85] He also mentioned the problems of people that the Rhodesian Government had driven into 'protected or collected villages', growing numbers of refugees in urban centres and in neighbouring countries, less food production, hunger and starvation, breakdown of health services and lack of veterinary services. He also noted that the war situation had given rise to lawlessness due to the abundance of weapons made available to people.

Archbishop Chakaipa also noted that quite apart from these hardships, the war had caused untold bloodshed and many thousands of innocent people had either died, or had been left crippled. 'It is this horrifying toll which causes our major concern and is the main reason for our approach', he concluded.[86] Observing that the Church delegation tended to view the armed struggle as another problem rather than a means to solving the problem of racism, Joshua Nkomo opened the discussion by asking the Church party, whether they had any solutions. From the discussions that ensued a suggestion was made to the effect that, 'the guerrillas might concentrate on the Security Forces and installations and try to avoid contact with the civilian people'.[87]

The Church party also took the opportunity to express concern about the violence against and murder of missionaries. By this time nineteen missionaries had died under suspicious circumstances.[88] The ZAPU president assured the Church delegation that under no circumstances had any orders been given by the leadership for murder or harrasment of missionaries. However, he felt obliged to further explain:

If the Patriotic Front forces have been guilty of this, blame the system, the war, the frustration, ill-discipline and possibly the fact that the Church has, in the past, supported or accepted the system.[89]

The ZAPU leadership assured the Church leadership that the Church was welcome in the new Zimbabwe and that she would be allowed to continue with schools and hospitals. However, regarding mission farms Joshua Nkomo appeared to be less unequivocal. He could only say that the State would spare those that were well utilised.[90]

At the end of the meetings between the Church delegation and the ZAPU leadership the former had become more convinced of the need for their involvement in trying to end the war. They assured the ZAPU leaders that there were certain areas in which the Church could give practical assistance immediately. These included finding assistance for refugees, (that is clothing, food and medical supplies); locating the parents of refugee children in Zambia and informing them; impressing upon whites that they were accepted by the Patriotic Front as Zimbabweans and persuading the interim government leaders to attend an all party conference.[91]

### Meeting with the ZANU leaders

Having completed their meetings with Joshua Nkomo and ZAPU representatives, the team from the Bishops' Conference and the commission went on to meet the ZANU leadership on the 20 and 21 August 1978 in Lusaka. The ZANU delegation comprised Robert Mugabe (President), Simon Muzenda (Chairman), Josiah Tongogara (Military Commander), Edgar Tekere (Secretary General) and Emmerson Mnangagwa (Security).

Sr Janice McLaughlin rightly observes that the Church party had learnt some diplomacy from their meeting with the ZAPU leaders.[92] They saw the need of modifying their opening statement to the ZANU leadership. The essence of the statement to the ZAPU leadership was maintained, highlighting the violence of the struggle for liberation, and the suffering brought to bear upon the ordinary people of Zimbabwe, and upon the Church. This statement was, however, made longer by the addition of two paragraphs that focussed on the role of the Church in condemning oppressive legislation since 1969. It also referred to missionary deportations, closure of schools, hospitals and withdrawal of missionaries from sensitive areas as a result of continued victimisation instilled by the Government on the Church because of its solidarity with the oppressed people of Zimbabwe. The statement amounted to an *apologia* for the Church's positive role in the country.

Compared to the first statement, this amended presentation even more highlighted the escalating violence in the country, the apparent coercion of the people to join the struggle, abductions and atrocities against missionaries. All this violence, Archbishop Chakaipa argued, was contributing to the withdrawal of Church personnel and the closure of institutions that had, for decades, been of great service to the people in the countryside.[93]

In his response, Mr Robert Mugabe the head of the ZANU delegation, expressed his gratitude for the deep concern which the Church was showing in making the visit to Lusaka. He noted the anxiety that the bishops and the JPC expressed regarding the security situation and the loss of life in the country. Mugabe directly focussed his response to the violence that the Bishop had spoken about. His concern, however, was whether violent revolution was justified.

Mugabe referred to the history of the struggle for liberation from the late 1950s to 1978. He stressed that for many years the nationalists had fought through non-violent means, but failed to achieve the desired results. The Rhodesia Front government, Mugabe argued, was maintaining itself by violence. This had led the nationalists to wage an armed struggle as a way of defending the majority of Zimbabweans. Hence, according to the Patriotic Front which was waging the armed struggle, the war they were fighting was just. He called upon the Church to understand their position.[94]

Commenting on the abduction charge, Mugabe insisted that the Patriotic Front forces had been instructed to persuade rather than coerce the people to join the struggle. The Rhodesian regime, he noted, accounted for more atrocities, since in their attempt to keep up the morale of their war machine, they killed even the collaborators and announced that they were guerillas. These atrocities against ordinary people often resulted in the latter fleeing the country into neighbouring countries.

In exactly the same way as Joshua Nkomo, Mugabe unequivocally stated that it was not tenable to reduce pressure of the war, as this would only lengthen it. In spite of their insistence on the need for persuasion, the ZANU delegation emphasised that suffering was part of the war; there was no way it could have been eliminated.[95]

The ZANU delegation, however, agreed that there were cases of indiscipline within their forces. Mugabe appealed to the Church delegation to 'assist by letting them know in which areas this was happening'.[96] The ZANU leaders assured the Church that action would be taken against misbehaving guerillas.[97]

On the role of the Church in the struggle, Mugabe noted that she had gone along with 'the system' in the past. However, with time, she had chosen 'the right path'. He particularly referred to the work of the Justice and Peace

Commission which he argued was 'well-known and appreciated'. Mugabe called on the Church to keep missions and other institutions open as far as possible. This was an indication that the Church was welcome in the new Zimbabwe to continue its work with the people. He also commented on Church-State relationships in the new Zimbabwe by saying that the Church would be required to take guidance from the government in the fields of education and health.[98]

The meeting between the representatives of the Church and the Patriotic Front leaders marked an important turning point in the history of the Church in Rhodesia. Previously, the Church had only asked for such 'meetings of concern' with the Rhodesian government leaders. The mere meeting with Ian Smith and his Ministers of Home Affairs and Defence was a recognition of the legitimacy of the Rhodesian government. But by 1978, the tide had turned. It was time to acknowledge the legitimacy of the Patriotic Front as the government-in-waiting. Apparently, the future of the country and Church was understood to lie with the Patriotic Front.

For the first time in six years of the armed struggle, the Church hierarchy got a feeling of oneness of purpose with the guerrilla leaders and the people at home. The mere thought that the Church delegation suggested to the Patriotic Front that their forces could lessen civilian peoples' suffering by concentrating on the security forces and Government installations sounded very revolutionary and affirmative to the guerrilla leaders. By meeting the Patriotic Front leaders and by suggesting a humanization, and not the termination of the armed struggle, the Church delegation had taken a step further than merely accusing the Rhodesian government of being largely responsible for the injustices which provoked the war. They had in fact taken a bold step in favour of the liberation struggle.

More than merely condemning the Government, the Bishops and the Commission were now secretly going out to meet the guerrilla leaders just as the small Christian community members, priests, sisters and brothers were secretly meeting guerrillas and consulting with them about the war in war-stricken zones. This meeting in Lusaka completed the circle of support for the liberation of Zimbabwe by the Church. Janice McLaughlin is correct in her observation when she says, 'If the Government thought that by removing Lamont they could silence the Church, they had seriously miscalculated'.[100]

With or without Lamont, the Bishops' Conference and the JPC had become a fearless critic of the Rhodesian Government and an unflinching supporter of the liberation cause.

From the Lusaka meeting of August 1978 began a working relationship between General Josiah Tongogara and Brother Fidelis Mukonori who was assigned by the JPC to cover 'complaints' regarding the guerrilla forces' behaviour in war zones. 'He would carry out on-the-spot investigations of any negative reports about the guerrillas and feed them back to the senior ZANLA Commander.'[101]

Reporting complaints to the ZANLA leadership became one of the three tasks that the Church leaders and the Commission undertook since the Lusaka meetings. The other two tasks were to meet internal leaders in an attempt to influence the peace process, and to establish ways of assisting refugees in neighbouring countries. These two are very well documented by Janice McLaughlin in her doctoral thesis.[102]

## Other operations

The Justice and Peace Commission thus later met the four internal members of the Executive Council of the Transitional government set up after the accord of 3 March 1978. In all its meetings with the nationalists, the Commission addressed the issue of violence and the need for reconciliation as the new political order was certainly dawning. Nothing positive emerged from the meetings, however.

After the elections in April, 1979 which excluded the Patriotic Front, the Commission condemned the Muzorewa government as a puppet regime. They went on to lobby at the Lusaka Commonwealth Heads of Government Meeting (CHOGM) in May 1979 not to recognise the regime. The Commission appealed for an all-party-conference as the only way for the country to gain peace and stability. As a force for reconciliation the Commission was also represented by brother F Mukonori and brorther Arthur Dupuis at the Lancaster Conference from September to December 1979, when finally a constitution for future independent Zimbabwe was drawn up.[105] The Commission had therefore, since 1974, become a mouthpiece of the oppressed, and especially of the rural majority which was shouldering the brunt of the repression from the Rhodesian forces and violence from the guerrillas.

## Overall assessment

In its latter days the Justice and Peace Commission made known the plight of Zimbabweans to the international community through lobbying at conferences. The Commission was supported by the Bishops' Conference in all these endeavours. The direction of Bishop Lamont (1974–77) and that of Helmut Reckter, the then Prefect of Sinoia, was significant throughout the period.

The cooperation between the JPC and the RCBC in championing the cause for justice and peace signified a new perception of the mission to preach the Gospel which demanded a radical commitment for the integral liberation of the human being. This new perception created an antithesis to the too easily unquestioned, fideistic perception which considered the activities of the Church as restricted within the four walls of a Church building or to the sacristy. So far many people, black and white were interested in the Gospel, but totally uninterested in applying it to the social and ethical problems of the country. The Bishops had become more alert to the new demands of the social teaching of the post-conciliar Church. Through involvement with those leading the struggle for liberation the Church made a more noticeable attempt to teach a new theology based on moral rather than dogmatic foundations.[106] The Church in Rhodesia had expanded its ecclesiological outlook. In fact the Commission was able to broaden its appeal to grassroots Catholics who, previously had been active in the Catholic Association, and now gave local support to the freedom fighters.

In spite of its appeal to the ordinary people since 1974, the Justice and Peace Commission however, failed to devolve its operations from the national office in Salisbury to the grassroot Christian communities. The amendments to the Commission's constitution made at the end of 1974 did not bear much fruit. The so-called 'long-term programme for African Adult education based on the conscientisation methods of Paulo Freire,'[107] did not get off the ground. Of course, the situation of insecurity in the rural areas made such a programme impracticable. But the urban dwellers could have benefited from this programme had there been both moral and financial support from the Bishop's Conference. The financial threshold never improved, so the programme was not implemented.[108]

The failure to have viable diocesan commissions, and parish committees, in the long run adversely affected the operations of the JPC in its endeavour to have a national programme. All the work which was supposed to be handled by the parish and diocesan structures was thrust upon the national office, thus stretching its capacity. This also affected the financial capacity of the national office. The Commission depended almost solely on overseas support. A negligible fraction was provided by the RCBC.[109] Financial dependence on overseas donors and not on the local constituency reflected on the Commission and the RCBC's poor marketing strategy in creating a sense of 'ownership' among local Catholics and other concerned citizens of Zimbabwe.

The Justice and Peace Commission's witness to social justice and peace was never carried to the family, the small Christian Community, the school, the work-place nor to social and civic life. This is the milieu within which Christians could have made specific and long-standing contribution to justice. Even the liturgy remained untapped for the local Church to better understand its Christian duty to work for justice and peace. The work for justice and peace remained the preserve of one organ of the Church. Nevertheless the Justice and Peace Commission had a significant impact on the Rhodesian political scene and indeed on the international community.

In his closing address to the Synod of Bishops on 30 September 1971, Pope Paul VI suggested action on behalf of justice and participation in the transformation of the world fully appear to us as constitutive dimension of the preaching of the Gospel or, in other words, of the Church's mission for the redemption of the human race and its liberation from every oppressive situation.[110]

Indeed, to embrace fully the goals of liberation and to work towards the transformation of the power structures that dominate the lives of a people in a given socio-political context, became the concern of the Church in Rhodesia in the period under study. However, it seems that as the Church became more and more involved in the socio-political life of the people it became less and less focussed on transferring power internally. In the way in which the new insights from Vatican II were implemented, there was, unfortunately, at significant points a breakdown of communication between the hierarchy, working in conjuction with the JPC and the local constituency. This state of affairs was to have repercussions after the struggle for independence.

## Notes

1. D Auret, *Reaching for Justice*, p.24.
2. Ibid.
3. RCBC Newsletter, No. 16., November, 1971, p.3.
4. Ibid.
5. Ibid., p.4.
6. Ibid. cf. also Minutes of the Consultative meeting at held at Chishawasha, on 20 November 1971. In Justice and Peace file of the General Secretariat Archives.
7. RCBC Newsletter, No. 17, December 1971, p.2.
8. Ibid.
9. Bishop A Haene of Gwelo diocese was president, while Messrs John Deary, Christopher Bishop, Sr Mary Aquina (OP), Fr J Elsener (SMB), Fr K Kinnane (OFM) and Peter Bunnett were members. Cf. JPC notes in Sr Janice McLaughlin's possession.
10. Ibid.

11. RCBC Newsletter No. 18, January 1972, p.13.
12. RCBC Minutes of the meeting held at Bulawayo from 17 to 19 January 1972. In RCBC General Secretariat Archives.
13. RCBC Newsletter, No. 30, January, 1973, p.33.
14. RCBC Newsletter No. 18, January, 1972, p.13.
15. RCBC Newsletter, No. 30. January 1973, p.34.
16. Ibid.
17. Ibid, p.41. Bishop Haene was president. The organizing Secretary was Brother Arthur (FMS) A J P Graham and Dr T O McLoughlin were the Chairman and Vice Chairman, respectively. The following were committee members, Mrs E M Rooney, Sr Mary Aquina Weinrich (OP), Fr E W Rogers (SJ), Mr E Muchena, Fr E Makusha, Mr F C Blackie, Mr John Deary, Mr and Mrs Zawaira, Sr Mary Linus (LCBC) and Mr S Maruza. An additional five members representing the five dioceses were, Messrs P Dougharty (Salisbury), P Oatley (Gwelo) G J Addeccott (Bulawayo), Rev E J O'Sharkley, and Rev G Prada (SMI) representing Umtali and Wankie respectively.
18. RCBC Newsletter No. 15, October, 1971. Cf. Appendix.
19. RCBC minutes of the meeting held on 15 January, 1973, p.10.
20. RCBC Newsletter No. 30, January, 1973, p 41.
21. Ibid.
22. RCBC Newsletter No. 50, October, 1974, p.2.
23. Ibid.
24. Linden, *The Catholic Church and the Struggle for Zimbabwe.* p.163.
25. Ibid.
26. Supra, p.189.
27. Linden, op.cit., p.195
28. RCBC Newsletter, No. 29, December, 1972, p.17.
29. RCBC No. 24, July, 1972, p.7.
30. Ibid.
31. Fr Pascal Slevin (OFM), Interview at Mt. St Mary's, Wedza, on 27 September. 1990.
32. RCBC Newletter, No. 24, July, 1972, p.7.
33. Ibid., p.9.
34. Ibid., p.9.
35. Ibid.
36. Ibid.
37. Ibid.
38. Ibid., p.8.

39. *Ibid.*
40. *Ibid.*, p.13.
41. *Ibid.*, p11.
42. *Ibid.*, p. 12.
43. *Ibid.*, p.9
44. Fr I T Makonese, Interview at Good Shepherd Church, Chiredzi, on 13 February, 1990.
45. RCBC Newsletter No. 24, July, 1972, p.10.
46. *Ibid.*
47. *Ibid.*
48. *Ibid.*
49. *Ibid.*, p.13.
50. *Ibid.*
51. T.O. McLoughlin 'Teaching the Laity: Some problems of the Christian Churches in Rhodesia', in A J Dachs, (ed), *Christianity South of the Zambezi*, Vol.1, p.192.
52. RCBC Newsletter, No. 24, July, 1972, p.9
53. *Ibid.*
54. *Ibid.*
55. The Land Tenure Act (1969) legislated for an Apartheid system of land distribution and population settlements. It demarcated land either 'European' or 'African'. Therefore an appropriate race had to occupy what was seemed 'appropriate' areas. Rekayi Tangwena rejected all efforts by the Authorities to evict him and his people from Gaeresi farm which had been demarcated European. The long-drawn dispute led to a lot of destruction of property and impoverishment of the Tangwena people. Children suffered most.
56. RCBC Newsletter, No. 29, December, 1972, p.13.
57. Fr G Mordekai, Interview at Mabelreign Parish, on 12 October, 1992.
58. RCBC Newsletter, No. 29, December, 1972, p.13.
59. *Ibid.*, Cf. Linden, *op.cit.*, p. 211.
60. RCBC Newsletter No. 29, December, 1972, p.13.
61. *Ibid*, p.20.
62. R Randolph *Report to Rome* p. 117.
63. Transcript of UPI Telex, New York, 30 May, 1974. Cf. RCBC Newsletter, No.47, June, 1974, p.24.
64. RCBC Newsletter, No.58, June, 1975, p.5.
65. JPC *Man in the Middle*, May 1975.

66. JPC, *Civil War in Rhodesia*, October, 1976, p.1.
67. *Ibid.*, p. 93
68. T Sheehy, and Sudworth, (eds) *Speech from the Dock*, 1977 C.I.I.R. p.17.
69. *The Tablet*, 28 August, 1976, p. 846.
70. *Ibid.*
71. C Torres, 'Message to the Christians', in A. Kee (ed), *A Reader in Political Theology*, p. 146.
72. Fr X Marimazhira, Interview, 15 November, 1991.
73. D Auret, *op.cit.*, pp. 83-4.
74. Brother Fidelis Mukonori, Interview, at Prestage House, on 28 September, 1988. He took over as Acting Chairman of the JPC after John Deary's arrest in February, 1979.
75. *Ibid.*
76. Annex A of the official minutes of the meeting of the Church delegation and ZAPU leaders in the presence of President K Kaunda, August, 1978. In CCJP Archives.
77. RCBC Newsletter, No.84, October, 1978, p.6.
78. Cf. note 76.
79. *Ibid.*
80. *Ibid.*, p.3.
81. *Ibid.*
82. *Ibid.*, p.5.
83. *Ibid.*
84. *Ibid.*
85. Annex, B. of the official minutes of the meeting of the church delegation and ZAPU leaders. Cf. note 76.
86. *Ibid.*
87. *Ibid.*, p.6.
88. R H Randolph, *Dawn in Zimbabwe*, p. 220. Cf. also J. McLaughlin 'The Catholic Church and Zimbabwe's war of Liberation, 1972-80.' Ph.D. thesis U.Z. 1991. p.548. Now revised and published as J McLaughlin, *On the Frontline*, Harare: Baobab Books, 1996.
89. Annex B. cf., note 85.
90. *Ibid.*
91. J McLaughlin, *op.cit.*, pp. 147-8. (D.Phil thesis)
92. *Ibid.*
93. Annex B, Cf. note 85.

94. Minutes of Church leaders with ZANU leaders, Lusaka, August 1978. In CCJP Archives.
95. Ibid.
96. Ibid., pp 7-8. c.f McLaughlin, op.cit., p.150. (D.Phil thesis)
97. Minutes of meeting with ZANU leaders, Cf. note 94.
98. Ibid, p.6
99. Brother F Mukonori, at Prestage House, on 28 September, 1988.
101. Ibid., pp. 150-51.
102. Ibid., pp. 151-65
103. RCBC Newsletter, No. 84, October, 1978, p.6.
104. CIIR *The Rhodesian Election Campaign*, 1979.
105. Fr F Mukonori, Interview at Wadzanai Training Centre, on 23 August, 1993.
106. RCBC 'Road to Peace', 1978. This is an example of the Bishops' new theology founded on moral rather than dogmatic teaching.
107. RCBC Newsletter No. 52, December, 1974, p.2.
108. Fr F Mukonori, Cf. note 105.
109. Minutes of AGMs show this dependence on charitable institutions like CAFOD, CEBEMO, CARITAS, MISERIOR etc.
110. 'Justice in the World', in V Mainelli (compiler), *Official Teachings: Social Teachings*, p.285.

## Chapter 7

# The Justice and Peace Commission in Independent Zimbabwe (1980-85)

### Introduction
The dawn of independence in Zimbabwe ushered in a new political climate conducive to transforming a formerly racial society into a non-racial society. In an interview on 15 April 1980, the first Prime Minister of Zimbabwe, Mr R G Mugabe called upon all citizens to forgive their erstwhile enemies and enunciated reconciliation as the policy that his Government was going to adopt.[1] The war which had been waged in earnest since December 1972 had ravaged the country's economy and had brought untold suffering on communities and individuals alike. Consequently, the Government of Mr Robert Mugabe pledged to steer the country towards peace, rehabilitation, reconstruction and the development of a better economic environment for the nation.[2] It is with reference to this new political dispensation and expectation gripping the country in 1980 and beyond that we pursue a critical evaluation of the operations of the Justice and Peace Commission after independence as an additional illustration of how the Catholic Church in Zimbabwe applied itself to the social ethics from the Second Vatican Council.

### The Roman Catholic Church's vision of the future
The important factor to consider when evaluating the work of the Justice and Peace Commission, after independence is the continued reflection of the leadership of the Roman Catholic Church in Zimbabwe on the social and political ministry of the local church, specifically focussing on the Bishops' Conference. The latter's thinking provide the matrix within which to understand the policies and operations of the JPC in particular and the rest of the episcopal commissions in the country. It is necessary to refer to some official statements produced by the Conference on behalf of the Catholic Church in Zimbabwe.

### ZCBC's statement on Independence Day
In a statement to mark the Independence of Zimbabwe[3] the Catholic Bishops' Conference congratulated all the citizens and the newly elected Government.

They took the opportunity to teach about the importance of guaranteeing the rights and duties of the individual and of communities. The Bishops pledged 'whole-hearted cooperation and support in the difficult but rewarding task of nation-building...'[4] They went on to qualify the cooperation they envisaged by referring to independence and autonomy between the Church and State:

> While the State and the Church are independent and autonomous in their own spheres, both are at the service of man. Their duty is to help man fulfil his personal and social vocation. The more they cooperate, the more effectively will they serve the good of all citizens. In this respect the Church and State are at the service of the country.[5]

The Bishops spelt out further the relationship between Church and State arguing that the former is not identified with any political system. Rather, they argued, the Church's function is to be the 'moral conscience of the nation, the sign and safeguard of the supreme value of the human person'.[6]

Drawing upon the past experiences during the UDI era, they rejected the dichotomy often made of political and church matters. They concurred with the Church's critics that the Church must be in a position to preach the faith and carry out her mission unhindered. They, however, added an element often ignored by the Church's, critics which is, that the Church, must be in a position to make moral judgements, even on political matters, when fundamental human rights on the salvation of men require it.'[7]

In this way they applied what they had learned from the Second Vatican Council, and subsequent post-Conciliar documents. Focusing on the importance of peace in the country the Bishops argued that upholding peace among people to the glory of God was an integral component of the Church's faith to the Gospel and a way of fulfilling her mission to the world. They, therefore, urged Christians to unite with all peace-loving citizens and to work for, and bring about peace:

> True peace cannot be achieved unless personal values are safeguarded, with men (sic) freely and confidently sharing their creative gifts. In building peace, respect for others and the determination to live as brothers are essential.[8]

This Independence statement served as a reminder, to the whole nation, of the basic civil duties and rights of citizens, the task of the Church in nation building and the Church's prophetic role in society at large. This teaching was to provide guidelines and parameters within which to evaluate the Church's work in independent Zimbabwe. This policy statement, we submit, had direct bearing on the operations of the Justice and Peace

Commission in particular. It was of course immediately related to what transpired during the final transition from colonial rule to independence.

The desire for justice and peace appear to have been some of the major expectations that the Bishops had as the country was entering a new political era. The two terms not only appear in the statement referred to above, but also in Archbishop Patrick Chakaipa's prayer to bless the Zimbabwean flag. At midnight of 17 April, 1980, Archbishop Chakaipa prayed for, 'those in authority... so that all their decisions may promote peace and common good.'[9] He also prayed for integrity of the citizens of Zimbabwe 'so that amid harmony, justice and peace, our country may enjoy true prosperity'.[10]

That Archbishop Chakaipa played the official role of blessing the flag was significant; a new chapter in Church-State relations in Zimbabwe was being written. At the time of the Pioneer Column's settlement at Salisbury, it was the Anglican Church that played a more public role. Since then, and throughout the period of colonialism, the Anglican Church was, if not formally so, at least informally the 'Establishment Church'.

On the eve of Independence, Prince Charles on behalf of Her Majesty the Queen handed to President Canaan Banana the constitutional instruments. However, instead of an Anglican Church prelate blessing the new Zimbabwe flag, it was the Roman Catholic Church Archbishop who performed that function. The Churches' roles and preferences during the liberation struggle may have determined the church which was to carry out the official business at Independence. It is also likely that the church to which the new Prime Minister belonged was considered the right choice considering the 'progressive' role that the Justice and Peace Commission of the Catholic Church had played during the liberation struggle.

Two nights before Independence, Robert Mugabe the new Prime Minister, had talked on Zimbabwean television of 'our hero Fr Jerry O'Hea', a Jesuit missionary and added, 'I suppose I am what Catholics have made me'. Although he had used an ominous phrase to the effect that, 'the war was a greater church than the Catholic Church', Mugabe also talked of the need for 'harnessing the Church and making it our partner.'[11]

At 8:30 am on Independence Day, Robert Mugabe, his mother, Mrs Bona Mugabe, his wife Sally, and his two sisters Sabina and Bridget attended a thanksgiving Mass for the birth of the new nation at the Catholic Cathedral in Harare. President Banana and Mrs Janet Banana also attended. Archbishop Patrick Chakaipa was the chief celebrant and was assisted by sixty-nine priests from the Salisbury Archdiocese. Representatives of all parishes in the Archdiocese and all religious congregations working in the diocese attended.[12] The Apostolic delegate and Charge d'Affaires as well as three Anglican bishops from Zimbabwe also attended.[13] An overseas reporter to the *Catholic Herald* wrote. 'Now the Marxist wolf had come in from the wilderness into their (Catholic's) fold. Was he a lamb — one of God's people like them after all?[14]

This event has symbolic significance in terms of the general Church-State relationship in the new Zimbabwe. It also marked the beginning of a fairly close relationship between the leadership of the Roman Catholic Church in Zimbabwe and Robert Mugabe and his Government. This relationship became an important factor in the tripartite relationship between the Government, the Justice and Peace Commission and the Zimbabwe Catholic Bishops' Conference, in the period under review.

## A new era in the Commission's role

### A new context

The Justice and Peace Commission had been founded and its constitution expressly devised for the situation in which the Church found itself in the 1970's in opposition to the politics of enforced racial segregation imposed by the Government of Rhodesia. The Lancaster House Constitution, to which the ZANU (PF) Government had pledged to commit itself, was the reverse side to the 1970 constitution; the latter promoted non-racial policies, while the former promoted racial segregation. The political situation was different in 1980 from that of 1971/2. It was imperative to transform the Commission in line with the political and social transformation that the country was going through.

The JPC therefore carried out a process of consultation throughout the whole of 1980 as a way of determining the new role it was to play. Of particular significance in shaping the Commission's new role were contributions from the Better World Movement, the 1980 Annual General Meeting, of the JPC and the 1980 Bishop's Administrative Meeting. We consider these in turn.

### The impact of the Better World Movement

The Better World Movement (now Church in the Service of the World) which was led by the former Director of the National Pastoral Centre, Fr Tim Page, played the lead in trying to transform the Commission towards a new role. The movement coordinated and facilitated weekend meetings for the executive members to plan for the future and to redefine the objectives of the organisation in the light of their faith and the changed circumstances in Zimbabwe.

Out of a series of meetings the JPC executive therefore formulated some of the objectives of the Commission as follows;

(i) to promote peace and justice through reconciliation of all people by the liberation and development of every man, the teaching of evangelical values and education for awareness, thereby raising the dignity of man;
(ii) to ensure that as a group we live justice and peace through personal relationships and awareness; that this spreads to our personal lives, and that our organisation involves more local groups;
(iii) to equip members to meet the main tasks of the Commission through studies at seminars and days of reflection.[15]

The above reveal one major concern which had been the Commission's shortcoming in the past, that is, the need to communicate with the rank and file within their local community on the importance of justice and peace. These objectives were not new, but merely a further amplification of one of the original aims of the Commission. In effect what the Better World Movement achieved through the series of seminars with the executive members was to help them re-prioritise the work of the Commission. Unlike the time of the war when it was difficult to meet and involve many people, especially in the rural areas, now the time was conducive for an educational awareness programme to be carried out nationwide.

## The Annual General Meeting of the JPC (September, 1980)

Although the Better World Movement weekend seminars helped significantly in the planning for the future by the Executive, the Commission was yet far from having a consensus opinion. Some thought that there was need to change the organisation's aims in line with the changed situation.[16] There appears to have existed a general euphoria with independence especially in 1980 when there existed a feeling that all was well since there now existed the 'government of the people'. Furthermore, the peace (that is, absence of war) that the country had acquired tended to make many formerly active members complacent.[17]

In fact, certain quarters had expressed ideas of bringing together the JPC and the (Catholic) Commission for Social Services Department (CSSD).[18] Apparently, these quarters were now prepared to forswear the JPC's specific role of promoting and developing an informed consciousness of justice and peace. Rather, they were prepared to harness all the Church's Commissions towards the 'development' of the country. Ironically, however, they failed to see the integral role of justice and peace in development and liberation. These were some of the issues that the Justice and Peace Commission Annual General Meeting had to attend to.

## CHAPTER 7 — Justice & Peace Commission in Independent Zimbabwe (1980–85)

The JPC Executive invited President Canaan Banana to address the Commission's AGM on this controversial issue — the role of the Justice and Peace Commission in independent Zimbabwe. In his address, President Banana stressed that in the post-war era of reconstruction, the Justice and Peace Commission, together with the rest of the Church, could make a meaningful contribution towards the development of the country. Of note, however, in Banana's view was the need for the Church always to exercise its prophetic role in society. This, Banana called the 'watchdog role':

> The 'watchdog' role of the Church remains relevant even in this changed situation. But careful study of Government policy is essential to constructive criticism and advice. The Church, in this respect, cannot afford to institute itself as a group in opposition to the wishes of the people as represented and symbolised by the Government.[19]

It seems, from this quotation, however, that President Banana was not ready for prophecy capable of taking free reign possibly against the thinking of the majority. What he was ready to accept, was a 'prophecy' qualified by the political majority whose prerogative could be reduced to 'constructive criticism and advice' vis-a-vis the Government. This thinking was not peculiar to Banana as we shall see later. Let us, however, find out what the participants to the Annual General Meeting felt about this ascribed role and the future of the Commission in general.

In the resolutions of the meeting the delegates from all six dioceses felt strongly that the Commission had a great role to play in the new Zimbabwe. The majority felt that the aims as laid down in the JPC Constitution (1972) provided a sound basis for the activities of the Commission, even in the new Zimbabwe. The change that the majority wanted to see was in terms of broadening the areas of activity in the dioceses.[21] More than simply getting to diocesan committees, what most participants wanted to see was a form of decentralisation that would affect the 'local church' at the grassroots. It was viewed as important 'to study their (grassroots communities) situation ... bearing in mind the social teaching of the Church and the government's social programme'.[22] In spite of the euphoria we referred to earlier, it is interesting to note that some participants had already noticed that certain Government authorities by virtue of their high and demanding positions were far removed from 'the little things that may bring peace to the grassroots'.[23] The participants concurred that it was in such situations that the Commission could be a particularly useful instrument in bringing peace to the grassroots communities.

The participants to the AGM took time to reflect on President Banana's address. They agreed that the role of the Commission was that of a 'watchdog'. However, the meeting added that the watchdog must be one that acts when action is called for. In other words the Church should not merely be watching.[24] The meeting agreed with Banana that there were numerous areas in the Government's development exercise that needed watching, studying and constructive criticism. Although the country enjoyed peace, in the sense that the war was over, the meeting noted that peace did not simply mean the absence of war. True peace, the AGM argued, touched on the economic, social, religious/spiritual and political spheres. All these factors brought about a 'peace of mind' which they considered as important.[25] In this regard they concurred with Pope Paul VI.

There was acrimony between some of the diocesan representatives, and the executive members regarding the structure of the Commission. These representatives favoured the bringing together of the JPC and the Commission for Social Service and Development (CSSD) at diocesan levels. The basis of this position was the recognition that the CSSD had well developed structures and links with the grassroots in its relief work. The JPC could, therefore, work along these structures. However, although these structural changes were proposed, they were not accepted by the majority. The Executive, however, decided to consult the Bishops' Conference on this issue.[26]

### A new voice from the bishops

In September, 1980, immediately after the annual general meeting of the JPC the bishops held an administrative meeting at which they called for the re-examination of the Commission's constitution. In their view the 1972 constitution was devised 'expressly for the situation in which the Church found itself in opposition to the politics of enforced segregation imposed by the Government of Rhodesia.'[27]

The Bishops registrered their appreciation of the work that the JPC had done during the liberation struggle. They noted that, members of the Commission had found themselves in opposition to the minority European Rhodesian Government in a difficult and dangerous situation.[28]

In their evaluation of the Commission's work which they viewed as 'largely successful'[29] the Bishops furthermore commended the courage of the executive members and the generous moral and financial support given by the many overseas agencies who supported the struggle for Justice and Peace in Zimbabwe.[30]

It is interesting to note, however, that the Bishops when reviewing the work of the JPC did not mention the moral and financial support that came form the local Church. This was probably an implied critique of the lack of local base for the Commission. This point is supported by the Bishops' urgency in setting up a committee that they tasked with the responsibility to draw up a new constitution. They demanded that this new constitution establish a direct relationship between the commission and the Bishops' Conference 'in order to give a greater role and responsibility to the diocesan committees'.[31]

The constitutional committee was chaired by Bishop Lamont, who had returned to Zimbabwe for a short period. Father Richard Randolph, the then Secretary General of the Bishops' Conference and Michael Auret, then Chairman of Commission were members. Again, only white Catholics were deemed to have the appropriate expertise for the assignment. Due to the short period that Bishop Lamont was in the country, the committee expeditiously inserted new proposals' into the old constitution. These changes were approved by the Bishops' Conference in December, 1980 for one year after which necessary alterations were to be made.[32]

## A new constitution for JPC (December 1981)

The new constitution for the Justice and Peace Commission took effect from 1 December 1981 after having been accepted by the Bishops' Conference at their annual general meeting on 9 November 1981. Henceforth the task of the former executive committee was terminated as members of a new executive were appointed. The commission effectively became the Catholic Commission for Justice and Peace (CCJP) changing from the Justice and Peace Commission. For the first time in the history of the Commission, an African Bishop, Patrick Mutume was appointed president. An African Director Mr Clement Mhondoro, took over from Mr John Stewart. The Chairmanship was, however, given to a white man, Mr Michael Auret, who took over from another very distinguished white man, Mr John Deary.[33]

The 1981 Constitution was however largely a reformulation of the 1972 constitution. It geared the CCJP towards the rehabilitation of the majority African people of Zimbabwe. It was expressly designed to redress the past imbalance in power-distribution between black and white members of the laity and between the top sectors and the grassroots in the Church. It therefore, stressed the need for the commission to have a preponderance towards indigenous Zimbabweans within the Executive.[34] This shift was considered to be particularly important:

> since the work of the CCJP must always be grounded in the people, especially those who, for whatever importunate reason, may remain poor and oppressed in their individual circumstances.[35]

Under the new constitution and in a new political dispensation where the Catholic Church enjoyed good relations with the Government, the Bishops' Conference stressed the need for the CCJP 'to carry out its role of constructive criticism of Government'.[36] In practice what this really meant was that the Commission 'must at all costs preserve a prudent degree of independence, and transcend party politics.[37]

Through the CCJP and other Commissions like the Catholic Social Service and Development, the Bishops' Conference viewed the Catholic Church as continuing without interruption but with continual adaptations to new situations, in its positive work for justice, peace and development in Zimbabwe, that is, in pursuit of the new ecclesiological and socio-ethical insights from the Second Vatican Council.

One major constitutional difference between the JPC and the CCJP was that the former operated semi-independently of the Rhodesia Catholic Bishops' Conference. Although it had a Bishop-President its decisions and pronouncement did not necessarily reflect the thinking of the Bishops' Conference.[38] From 1981, however, the CCJP was to be under the Bishops' Conference. On this issue the Bishops' Conference had consulted Rome. And so on 9 November 1981, this specific wish was supported by the Sacred Congregation for the Evangelisation of Peoples through the Apostolic Nuncio.[39]

The Bishops argued that the CCJP should maintain the same aims and objectives that the JPC had been formed to achieve. What was being changed, however, were the methods for achieving these aims and objectives. The new methods that the Bishops' Conference recommended, it seems, did not go down well with the executive members of the old Commission. The Bishops' decision to have the Commission operate directly under the responsibility of the Bishops' Conference was viewed as a curtailment of the lay people's decision-making role in the Church. Furthermore, the move was also viewed as a manifestation of episcopal authoritarianism that was aimed at eliminating diversity in the thinking and actions within the Church.[40]

After reformulating the constitution, the Bishops' Conference invited:

> those who served under the previous constitution with such distinction ... to consider whether they would be willing to serve in terms of the new constitution.[41]

As already noted above, no one from the old executive were willing to serve; they all stepped down in protest, and as a sign that they had found the terms undesirable. Whether or not the new constitution afforded the Commission the latitude to operate more expeditiously afterwards can only be judged after analysing its work.

## CCJP and decentralization: A new way of operation

One major reason expressed by the Bishops' Conference for reformulating the JPC was the need to encourage indigenous Zimbabweans to take an active part in the the Commission's work. This was viewed as being in line with 'the increased number of indigenous bishops in the Conference' and indeed with the new emphasis on the local church.[43] In 1981 the Conference consisted of three African bishops and three white bishops.

In his first address to the Commission, the Chairman of the new Executive Committee Michael Auret, gave more or less the same emphasis that the Bishops had made. In his first address to his executive he stressed:

> The Church is asking us to help in bringing peace through justice to the poor in the first place and then all the way up the social strata. I therefore think that our first duty is, as it were, to climb down to the grassroots; to study their situation in our society bearing in mind the social teaching of the Church and the government's social programme.[44]

The national executive committee, at the end of the meeting, resolved to 'expand and consolidate the diocese work and to encourage the formation of parish level committees'.[45]

## Visits to dioceses by the National Office

Through regular visits to dioceses the Director of the CCJP in the course of 1982, saw some useful contacts being made with some parishes. Sinoia prefecture and Gwelo, Umtali and Wankie dioceses had, by the end of the year, diocesan committees on justice and peace which met regularly.[46] After a lot of encouragement, even the Bulawayo diocesan committee became more and more active. A problem remained in the Salisbury Archdiocese. In spite of the national executive being located in the Salisbury Archdiocese, there was very little preparedness to set up a diocesan committee and still less parish committees.[47] By 1982 only two parishes, one in Sinoia prefecture and another in Gwelo diocese had decided to study and discuss the social teaching of the Church.[48]

From 1983 to 1985, the national office undertook to visit diocesan committees more often. The office not only paid visits and facilitated discussions on the Church's social teaching and human rights but also provided diocesan committees with literature, topics for discussion and other materials related to issues of justice.

## Education for Justice and Peace: The Gweru Seminar (February 1982)

The need to promote education for justice and peace in the Church is one major emphasis that emerged since the adoption of the new constitution. This education for justice programme was launched with a seminar in Gweru from 5 to 6 February, 1982. Three papers were presented, namely 'The Social teaching of the Church', 'Socialism in Zimbabwe' and 'Reconciliation'. The Prime Minister of Zimbabwe, Robert Mugabe, was the person who talked on socialism in Zimbabwe.

The Prime Minister's speech at this seminar was his first definitive statement on the form of socialism which his Government proposed for the country. According to the CCJP chairman, this speech afforded the Bishops' Conference and the whole Church in Zimbabwe the opportunity to study the Government's thinking on socialism and to consider the position of the Church in relation to the policies which were to be implemented in Zimbabwe.[49]

What was most interesting to the seminar participants was the similarity between the paper, the 'social teaching of the Church' presented by Sr. Hyacinth (O.P) and that on 'Socialism in Zimbabwe', presented by Mr Robert Mugabe, the Prime Minister. The participants' reaction to Mr Mugabe's speech was very similar to that of Archbishop Edward Cassidy, the Apostolic Nuncio to Zimbabwe.[50] After giving an opening address to the Inter-regional Meeting of the Bishops of Southern Africa on 2 June, 1980, the Nuncio drew attention to the apparent contradiction between the theory and the practice of the Socialism advocated for Zimbabwe by its government.[15] He had noted:

> The importance of the catecheses of social teaching was brought home to me rather forcefully in conversation with the new Prime Minister of Zimbabwe, Mr Robert Mugabe, when I heard defined as Marxist, social doctrines that seemed to me to be eminently Christian. Here was an able and learned African leader, with a Catholic background and education, having resort to Marxist teaching in order to be inspired by Catholic social principles.[52]

The reactions at the Gweru seminar regarding Mr Mugabe's speech on socialism, prompted the Catholic Church to investigate fully the type of socialism that the State was going to implement and the envisaged role of the Church in the new era. There was quite some concern in the Church; whether the Church was only going to be tolerated for so long, as it could help provide a motive for morality and a succession of golden eggs for development projects or whether she was wanted as part of the life of the

CHAPTER 7 — *Justice & Peace Commission in Independent Zimbabwe (1980–85)* 107

nation. Recommendations from such an investigation could generate a peace of mind in Church people when they clearly understood Government policy on religion. On concluding the investigation, a report produced in June 1982 by the General Secretariat of the ZCBC made several major points. The first was that Mr Mugabe, during his years of imprisonment lived as a devout Catholic:

> The turning point in his Catholic life may have been his entrance into Mozambique, where he found that ZANU/ZANLA had been formed by Marxist methodology, but not altogether by its ideology.[54]

The second was that Robert Mugabe did not appear to be a Marxist ideologue:

> The ZANU(PF) Government seeks the force that can help it establish a form of communalism, rather than communism in Zimbabwe; and enculteration compatible with the local people's traditions.[55]

The third was that a great deal of what the Prime Minister had to say came 'straight out of the pages of Vatican II, especially from *Gaundium et Spes* ...'[56]

The fourth was that although Mr Mugabe and his ministers so often referred to Zimbabwean socialism as being based on Marxist-Leninist principles, 'it may be that they do not necessarily mean to include the specifically anti-theistic, and therefore, anti-Christian principles.'

In conclusion the report assured the Church in Zimbabwe, that there was much to hope for since she was wanted as part of the life of the nation.[57]

## Conscientisation workshops

Following upon the Gwelo Seminar a series of 'conscientisation workshops' were organised by the National office, in order to increase awareness on issues of justice and peace, both at the national and the diocesan levels. However, since the Gweru seminar in February 1982, the CCJP National office became preoccupied with research and reporting on the security situation in South-Western Zimbabwe. The first national workshop was not held until October 1983 at Silveria House. Its aim was 'to assist the participants to think about justice and to work for justice and peace'.[59]

Again, because of the National office's preoccupation with the security situation in Matebeleland and parts of the Midlands, it took a long time to organise a follow-up workshop. From 11 to 13 January 1985, the second national workshop was held again at Silveira House. Its aim was to help the diocesan committees of the Catholic Commission for Justice and Peace 'to consolidate themselves and to become more widely known in their respective areas through whatever structures they chose to utilise'.[60] This workshop was not represented nationally as the previous one because there were no delegates from Harare and Bulawayo dioceses.

The third and final workshop within the period under study, was that held from 20 to 23 August, 1985. This was a very important workshop since it focused mostly on reports from the dioceses and at the end came up with an action plan to increase awareness of justice and peace in the country.

### A new emphasis on human rights

Another reason why this workshop was important was that it came immediately after the second general elections in the country. It therefore, provided an important opportunity for the participants to assess the human rights situation after the first five years of independence in Zimbabwe.

Reports from across this country expressed much concern with regard to religious freedom. They noted that in spite of the constitutional provision making specific reference to protection of freedom of conscience,[61] this had remained theoretical particularly during local and national election. The reports noted that during the national election campaign, people were forced to attend political rallies whose time clashed with that of Church services.[62] There had been cases reported to the CCJP offices where church services were disrupted by members of the ZANU(PF) Youth League.[63]

Another area of human rights violation that all dioceses reported was the interference with individual rights to privacy and family life. This had been found to be prevalent in high-density urban areas, mining and agricultural centres. People were reported as living in fear due to political intimidation. Connected with this interference was the lack of tolerance that the ruling party had of minority parties. The participants reported not only about lack of freedom of expression, association and peaceful assembly, they had also observed that the freedom of citizens was being judged, based on affiliation to a political party. This situation was prevailing in the whole country.[64]

This political intolerance and violations of the freedom of expression, association and assembly resulted in the failure to respect people's right to own property. This had been true particularly in the aftermath of the June 1985 election. Parts of Chitungwiza, and some high density suburbs in Harare, Kwekwe, and Gweru had been affected by this post-election violence.[65] The situation was exacerbated by the police, who were nowhere to be found when called upon to protect the human victims from this violence.

Some incidents of violence were believed to have been caused or with the knowledge of high-ranking members of both the ruling party and Government. In such situations the police found themselves shackled out of fear of victimisation by the said party or government officials. The country found itself therefore in a mess with, 'an irresponsible youth and police force who appear more answerable to the ZANU (PF) party than to their own parents and State.'[66]

The disturbances during and after the 1985 general elections, were just the tip of a cancer affecting the whole government system. According to the reports given at this workshop the condition laid for attaining a job in the Civil Service was a ZANU (PF) party card. Bulawayo, Harare and Chinhoyi diocese reported on such practices.[67]

Another issue that featured prominently concerned the security situation in Matebeleland. There were reports detailing the injustices and violations of human rights in the region. This was understandable, considering the backdrop of the dissident activities and the atrocities of the security forces in the region. Delegates from the Bulawayo diocese referred to the lack of freedom of expression and assembly in Matebeleland. They also reported on the intimidation of law-abiding citizens by 'enforcing agents' who would pick up anyone at gun point at any time.[68]

According to the Bulawayo diocese reports the people of Matebeleland were being labelled as 'dissidents'. Such labelling was viewed by the participants as flouting the brotherhood of people and had resulted in citizens regarding each other along tribal and partisan lines.[69] As a result the people of Matabeleland were living in perpetual fear and confusion as to the real identity of dissidents. The reports went on to point to the arbitrary arrest and detention for unspecified reasons, torture by the security forces and police, as well as disrespect for court verdicts by police and the Central Intelligence Officers (CIO).[70]

From this workshop, it was observed that politics was underlying most of the problems facing Zimbabwe since independence. The participants' explanation for this violence was that it stemmed from the fact that independence for the country had been attained through the barrel of the gun. Consequently, there had been an over-glorification of violent struggle and it was envisaged that people would take time to adjust.

The ruling party was viewed as not having sufficiently adjusted from violent to non-violent methods. Related to this was the leadership's desire to feel secure and to perpetuate their policies. This was seen as the probable reason why the ZANU (PF) party attempted to incorporate everyone within their ranks. Such hunger to stick to power sometimes resulted in intentionally or unintentionally joining forces with criminals.[71] It was this same hunger for power that the workshop identified as the explanation behind fighting in Matabeleland and the lack of dialogue between ZANU (PF) and PF-ZAPU. Winding up their analysis on the reports from the dioceses, the participants noted that in spite of shortcomings, the June 1985 elections proved to be a true reflection of the people's will.[72]

They finally drew up on action plan for the CCJP. The delegates expressed hope of establishing committees for justice and peace in all parishes. One possible way towards the attainment of this goal was through the national Justice and Peace office which had the capacity to facilitate deanery and parish seminars with relevant material. There was also a call for a massive education programme on human rights to be launched in colleges and schools. The delegates further called for the translation of the United Nations charter on human rights into local languages.[73]

The workshop thus ended on a high note, once again underscoring the importance of educating the people about their rights. It was hoped that what the delegates had learnt in this four-day workshop, the longest and most successful ever held, was going to stimulate much discussion and debate in the dioceses and parishes and would create greater awareness in justice and peace in the Church.

## The Justice and Peace newsletter: A new means of communication

The seminar of February 1982 saw the launching not only of the 'conscientisation workshops' but also of a post-independence newsletter, which was to become another instrument through which the Commission intended to attain the objectives of its role as 'watchdog' and promoter of 'education for justice'. The newsletter was meant among other things, to be 'the organ through which the committees and members throughout the country keep in touch with one another and exchange ideas'.[74] The national office expected to receive contributions to this newsletter, in the form of news of the committees' and members' work. Also, articles produced by diocesan or parish committees on relevant subjects were welcome.[75]

It was the national office that published the newsletter. However, since it was mainly aimed at the Catholic laity, it was distributed for sale through the diocesan Justice and Peace Committees, Missions and parish centres. The proceeds of 5 cents per copy was to go to the diocesan committees.[76] At the time of launching, in February 1982, the circulation of the newsletter stood at 3 000. The National office also sent the newsletter to Government and the news media.[77]

Five issues were sent out in 1982, with the first issues covering reports from dioceses that sent delegates to the Gwelo seminar and various talks

CHAPTER 7 — *Justice & Peace Commission in Independent Zimbabwe (1980–85)* 111

given at that seminar.[78] While 1982 appears to have been quite a success, considering the numbers of newsletters printed and sent out, 1983 was the year to evaluate the real break-through of this educational instrument. From the experience of the first two issues two major problems came to light. The first was described by the national chairman as, 'serious and disturbing, because if it is not solved satisfactorily, then the whole objective of publishing a people's CCJP newsletter would have been defeated.'[79]

This problem had to do with the distribution to parishes. The National office would send several copies of the newsletter to each parish priest in the country, in the hope that he would pass them on to his parish council for distribution, but more often than not, the parcel of newsletters from CCJP was relegated to:

> that 'useless' heap of literature that arrives at the desk of the busy parish priest uninvited and is either immediately condemned to the dust bin or is thrown into some obscure place where it is buried and never reaches the laity for whom it is primarily meant.[80]

The second problem had to do with the delay between giving the newsletter to the printers and getting it back ready for distribution. For instance, having distributed the first 1983 issue in August, the Commission immediately sent the second newsletter for printing with the aim of having it come out in November. However, they only got it back from the printers in mid-January 1984.[81]

The Commission could not do very much about these two problems. As for the first problem, the newsletter was meant to have been distributed by the diocesan committees through the parish cells (that is, the Small Christian Communities) or by parish representatives of the CCJP. While this would have been the most effective arrangement the reality was that the Commission had not effectively spread the gospel of justice and peace to the grassroots levels. The Commission soon realised this. Their only resort was to call for 'any ideas and suggestions from any quarter that might help in the effective distribution of the newsletter'. As for the second problem, the Commission found itself so powerless that it simply said that it 'was much beyond our executive's control'.[82]

More problems, however, beset the CCJP in 1984 and 1985. Only two editions of the newsletter appeared in 1984 followed by another two in 1985. This was partly due to the lack of staff in the National office, and also due to the 'total lack of contributions from the dioceses'. These reasons reduced the educational impact of the newsletter. These problems dampened the optimism of the national office at a time that they had increased the circulation from 3 000 to 3 500 and had changed printers.[84] One development that brightened their hopes, however, was the positive impact that their workshops seemed to have had on some parish priests. A few were becoming more and more interested in attending, and as a result the distribution and circulation of the newsletter became better. This created some hope that the newsletter would become effective on the laity.[85]

## The newsletter in the context of political turbulence: The crisis in Matebeleland

The coming of independence brought with it some problems and crises. Although the repatriation exercise and the disarming of combatants were generally successful, 'many thousands of weapons and explosives had been secreted in caches from which they could be recovered at leisure'.[86] The clashes between ZANLA and ZIPRA in late 1980 and early 1981 at Intumbane and Chitungwiza respectively led to growing mutual suspicion between ZANU(PF) and PF-ZAPU, the two major parties in the then 'coalition government' of unity. These clashes also undermined the steady progress that the national army was making in integrating the erstwhile opponents. Large scale defection of EX-ZIPRA officers from the army heading to the establishment of the fledgling 'dissident' movement started to occur at the end of 1981. This was followed by a bigger number of ZIPRA guerillas in February 1982, following the dismissal of Mr Joshua Nkomo and the arrest of PF-ZAPU members.[87] These defections led to swelling members of 'dissidents" already in existence in Matabeleland.

From as early as February 1982, reports expressing concern about the situation in Matebeleland were submitted to the commission. While at this early stage, reports centred on injuries and brutalities incurred at the hands of 'dissidents', from August and September 1982 complaints relating to the 'security measures' adopted by the army were received in increasing numbers.[88] As the dissident problem in Matabeleland continued and later spilt over into Midlands province, more and more suffering was brought to bear on ordinary people.

The CCJP spoke out and pleaded on behalf of the defenceless victims of this fighting, which in their view was politically motivated.[89] It increasingly expressed the earnest desire for the Church to address the root causes of the dissident problem as the first and necessary step in the process of bringing about lasting peace in the affected areas.

In its newsletter of November 1983, the CCJP regretted that since 1982 it had spent most of its time addressing itself to the side effects of the dissident problems, namely the suffering of the ordinary people in the affected areas. Its efforts had, however, remained limited because of lack of manpower. The CCJP had for some time been aware of the urgent need to address itself to the fundamental causes and reasons that brought about the dissident problem. To this end it had appealed to its members in the diocesan committees to work actively in this regard.[90]

In its newsletter of November 1984, the Commission called upon the churches of Zimbabwe to embark on some kind of peace initiative. Emphasis was, however, placed on getting to the root causes of the dissident activities prior to any such initiative:

> This entails the need to talk, either directly or indirectly through some intermediaries, with the dissidents in order to find out what exactly it is they are fighting for.[91]

The Commission went further to argue that the first and major problem in the way of any kind of initiative was that of communication with the dissidents. Without such communication, nobody would be able to establish objectively and authoritatively their reasons for taking up arms.[92]

In underscoring the importance of communicating with the dissidents, the CCJP argued that leaving them out would mean that whatever peace initiative was embarked upon would not make them obliged to or feel bound by the resultant agreement:

> We are appealing therefore, to all men of good will to help the churches to establish clearly what it is the dissidents are fighting for, so that in turn the churches will be in a better position to try and intermediate on behalf of peace in the country, without which only untold suffering and hardship will continue to be the lot of the people in the affected areas.[93]

## Election violence

In 1980, Zimbabwe had successfully carried out the first general election which was monitored by Commonwealth and other observers. As 1985 was approaching, the time had come for the first national elections to be run locally. The CCJP pleaded that they should be run in a free and fair environment. Five months away from the elections scheduled for March 1985, *The Herald* in its comment noted:

> As a young nation we directly need to set a precedent of clean, peaceful elections. If we miss this opportunity to set such a precedent, we shall have condemned future Zimbabwe to the disgrace and debauchery of violent elections for ever.[94]

This comment had to be understood within the context of politically motivated pre-election violence, that was already taking place in many provinces apart from the violence associated with dissidents and security forces in Matabeleland South, North and the Midlands provinces. The CCJP noted that since July 1984, political violence had erupted in major Midlands towns of Gweru, Kwekwe, and Zvishavane. There had been a change in the situation in the predominantly ZAPU areas, and even in the grey areas, that is, areas with substantial following of both ZANU(PF) and ZAPU. This change had to do with the increasing involvement of party youth in political violence.

ZANU (PF) youths were reported to have been forcing people to purchase party cards. In some cases they were reported to have forced bus travellers to purchase cards before allowing them to travel. Of greater concern to the nation were the reported alliances between the ZANU(PF) youths and the militia and Central Intelligence Officers (CIO) and total inactivity and ineffectiveness of the police.[97] Furthermore it had been established that the youth were being supported and sponsored by the ZANU(PF) party:

> And yet we know that the youth have often arrived at their destruction targets in buses, for which someone must have paid, and again perhaps some of the violence springs from rally speeches by other senior members.[98]

A typical case of party sponsorship of violence was reported in the February edition of the *Parade* magazine. The report noted that on 9 December 1984, the Governor of Matabeleland South, Mark Dube, addressed a ZANU(PF) rally at Dingumuzi Stadium in Plumtree:

> Among other things, he said that ZANU(PF) was a party with a clear direction and a known leader, not like Jesus whose father was unknown and was a son of a prostitute. At the conclusion of his speech he said Dingumuzi Township in Plumtree deserves to be burnt by fire. He then said he had brought bull-dogs to fix up the Plumtree people. 'Liyamazi ufezela na?', he asked (Do you know a scorpion?) The people answered 'Yes'. Then he said, 'You will feel his sting today'.[99]

This rally was followed by disturbances that left 200 victims who were treated at Plumtree hospital. Out of these, forty three were admitted as in-patients.[100]

Such ZANU(PF) motivated and sponsored violent disturbances, were not received passively by ZAPU or any other political parties. They sparked counter attacks which led to escalating violence. This is captured in an extract of a letter sent to the CCJP Chairman by a leading ZAPU supporter and Catholic from Matabeleland:

> The Matabele have for very many months now been subject to extreme provocation by bus loads of ZANU youth, travelling around the country, breaking up political meetings, burning homes, stoning cars, beating up people most brutally, all while protected by the army and police. The actions taken by ZANU thugs can only be likened to their Nationalist Socialist counterparts in Germany before the last world war. But they have seriously miscalculated their opponents. They are not as relative handful of peace-loving Jews amongst a sea of Germans, but a substantial portion of the population, an arrogant people with warlike forebears.[101]

Such were the sentiments of some Ndebele and ZAPU supporters. It was not surprising that some ZANU(PF) youths were murdered in the run-up to the general elections of 1985.[102]

In an attempt to arrest the prevailing inter-party violence, the Prime Minister, in February 1985, announced a postponement of elections from March to June, 1985. Although the CCJP welcomed the postponement, they emphasised that if serious steps were not taken to prevent the violence, it was going to increase as the elections were drawing near. As a concrete way to combat the inter-party violence, the CCJP decided to take advantage of the postponement of the elections by publishing a newsletter that would educate the public on the importance of national elections and the voting process. The newsletter came out in early June just a few weeks before the elections.

The CCJP appealed to voters to exercise their right to participate, through voting, in the decision making process in matters that affected their lives:

> Voting in a general election is a way of participating in deciding how the affairs of a country, which affect all citizens, should be run. For those who would like to see a change, it is the most peaceful and accepted way of effecting the desired change. For those who would like to keep the status quo, it is also, imperative that every individual capable of exercising their right should do so.[103]

The CCJP emphasised that voting was a peaceful way of self-expression and that a general election was very important. Consequently, the Commission argued, it was imperative that the right to vote be exercised after some careful consideration of the consequences of one's decision.

Apart from emphasising the importance of the right to vote, the newsletter appealed to the public to look at how they were to conduct themselves, both during the election-campaign and the election itself. Whilst the CCJP warned against those who could not care less whether they voted or not, they equally warned against those citizens, who were over-enthusiastic about elections to the point of disregarding higher rights, such as that of life.[104]

The newsletter also appealed to political leaders to refrain from inciting their members to violent behaviour:

> We believe that political leaders engaged in the campaign exercise would render real service to the community, if their speeches and talks paid more attention to enunciating party policy, and impressed upon their followers to refrain from all forms of violence.[105]

The media, both print and electronic, got a word of advice from the CCJP. The newsletter taught on the importance of press freedom during the campaign and the election times:

> Press freedom ..., plus fair and unbiased coverage of the campaign activities of all contesting parties, is a necessary recipe for free and fair elections. People have a right to information.[106]

Peace, the CCJP stressed, could only be achieved in a non-violent atmosphere where the ballot was cast freely. This newsletter was one of the CCJP's most familiar ways of contacting the general populace since independence. However, it was not easy to know the real effect it had on the public it addressed. What can be said with certainty is that the violence tailed off from the time that the Prime Minister announced the postponement of the general elections. The fears that the CCJP had of intense violence in the final run-up to the election were not realised. The first general elections since independence were carried out successfully and peacefully. 'The Commission congratulated the Government on this achievement, immediately after the elections'.[107]

Published just a few weeks before the elections, the newsletter with a print run of only 10 500 copies in English, Shona and Ndebele, could not have made much impact. Too short a time remained before the elections. The newsletter appeared only after the elections had been postponed which made it rather *ad hoc* and reactive rather than proactive. The publication of the newsletter could have been accompanied by a national workshop followed by diocesan, deanery and parish workshops or seminars with a focus on the grassroots communities. Such workshops and/or seminars would have been invaluable, especially to a voting public composed of people with basic literacy skills. Again such a programme would have required huge financial backing, to cater for travel and maintenance costs of members, of both the national office and diocesan committees. The financing of the Commission is the last area that we are going to consider.

CHAPTER 7 — *Justice & Peace Commission in Independent Zimbabwe (1980–85)* 117

## The financial state of the Commission

One of the weakness of the Justice and Peace Commission during the pre-independence period was its almost exclusive dependence on international donor agencies for its finances. Organisations and agencies like the International Defence Aid Fund (IDAF — London), Catholic Fund for Overseas Development (CAFOD — London), Central Agency for Joint Financing Development Programmes (CEBEMO-The Hague), Trocaire (Dublin) and many others, financed the operations of the Commission.[108] Finances running into tens of thousands of dollars were needed each year to finance the running of the national office, education and research programmes, publications and legal expenses.

The years 1972 to 1974, 1975 to 1977 and 1978 to 1980 were provided for by overseas donor agencies for the respective three year periods. However, with the coming of independence, the availability of funds from overseas became less definite.[109] Due to the cessation of fighting towards the end of 1979, the Commission with its new mandate managed to spend less in 1980, to the extent of remaining with some money in 1981.

By early 1981 the Commission was running out of funds. In July 1981, the CCJP therefore decided to send its acting Director to Europe to raise funds. The trip was, however, unsuccessful. The Commission was forced to revise its proposed budget before again sending its Chairman on another fund-raising tour to Europe in November, 1981. Although this attempt was more successful, the Commission got operating finances for only two years.

The failure of the first overseas trip was a lesson to the Commission. Although the Commission got the money after the second attempt at fund-raising, one important point was made: that every effort should be made to raise funds locally. To this end the Commission at its Annual General Meeting in February 1982, decided to approach the Bishops' Conference to allow the Commission to be the recipient of all collections in Zimbabwe on Peace Sunday. This Sunday was normally held at the end of January each year. Such collections, the Commission argued, could go towards the salary and expenses of diocesan coordinators.[110] When approached, the Bishops Conference welcomed the idea of supporting the Commission, arguing that it was long overdue and in line with the Church's policy of self-support which was adopted in 1973 under the Small Christian Community programme which we have already referred to in Part I.[111]

In the Annual Report for 1982, the Chairman noted that the Commission was:

> still completely dependent on overseas funds during 1982 and our overseas donors are beginning to ask whether the members of the Catholic Church in Zimbabwe care enough about justice and

peace in their country to provide at least some of the necessary funds for the Commission.[112]

The year 1982 saw the Commission, after adopting the new constitution, devoting a good deal of time to the formation and encouragement of diocesan committees. During this year the national office sent Zimbabwe $200.00 to each diocese for use by the diocesan committee once formed. The national office gave assurance to committees already in existence, that if they had particular projects or activities that required funding, they could get limited support. The national Commission understood its role at this stage as that of nurturing the diocesan committees, hence the importance of financing their activities. The hope was that in due course the dioceses would support themselves in all activities having to do with justice and peace.[113]

Sadly, in the 1983 annual report, the chairman was forced to repeat the observation made in 1982 concerning the financial resources of the Commission.[114] During this year, most overseas agencies agreed only to fund individual projects. They were refusing to fund salaries of diocesan coordinators. For instance, CAFOD agreed to sponsor the preparation and publication of the rights and duties pamphlets, while TROCAIRE provided a grant for the Commission to render legal aid to clients arrested or detained for reasons of a political nature. Similarly, CCFD sponsored the conscientisation programme which the Commission effected through the running of national workshops.[115] Evidently the insistence by overseas donors to sponsor specific projects was a way of keeping track of the use of their money by the Commission.

For the first time, however, the local bishops in Zimbabwe apportioned a paltry Z$200.00 each, of the proceeds from their diocesan Peace Day and Lenten Sacrifice Campaign towards the work of the Commission. Furthermore, individual and anonymous local donors also gave their small but valued donations. Although this local contribution could not even finance the ordinary budget for the national office, the Commission viewed it as a symbolic but significant gesture, which was given 'in the conviction that the Commission is carrying out a necessary and worthy mission in Zimbabwe'.[116]

In 1983 and 1984 the Commission ended up with deficits of Z$2 135.00 and $9 538.00 respectively. This was due to the expenses associated with its involvement in the Matabeleland crisis. Investigations of arrested and detained people, legal fees for attorneys and travel costs for researchers/investigators led to the deficit. This led the National office to stop assisting diocesan committees.[117]

In 1985 the Commission was back on the begging trip overseas. This became the norm for the organisation after having made insignificant impact on the local Church. 'Self support' has remained 'a pipe dream for the local Church especially for the Commission of Justice and Peace'.[118] This state of affairs continued even after 1985.

## Conclusion

With Independence, the Catholic Church in Zimbabwe entered into a new relationship with the State. It became a partner with the 'government of the people' in the struggle for a free and egalitarian Zimbabwe. This new relationship necessarily affected its formal organs specifically designed for promoting the social ministry of the local Church, that is, the Catholic Commission for Justice and Peace. Continued developments after 1980 are however contradictory. On one hand the CCJP became more closely integrated into and under the hierarchical structure of the Church. On the other hand, it managed, through topical seminars and a specially designed newsletter, to broaden its local base and encourage communication with the rank and file of local Catholics. Nevertheless the local financial base for the operations of the Commission continued to be frail. After 1980 this proved to be even more serious than before due to the new policy of overseas donor agencies that opted for direct support to individual projects rather than general grants for administration at national, diocesan and parish levels.

However, the Commission and the local church tried to pursue the concerns for justice, peace and human rights that had been promoted by the Second Vatican Council. The CCJP, through its diocesan committees, thus engaged in concrete projects and cases of injustice not only affecting Matabeleland but the county as a whole. It spoke out on behalf of victims of political intolerance and repression that gripped several communities due to political tensions. It certainly took outstanding courage for ordinary people to become members of the Commission for Justice and Peace. The political intolerance that was prevalent during the period under study, undermined the freedom of expression and assembly throughout the Zimbabwean of society. Even the Church was affected. The fear instilled in citizens indirectly, influenced the CCJP's efforts which aimed at enlisting grassroot membership and support in the fight for justice and peace. As a result, the workshops and seminars meant to conscientise the rank and file on the importance of building a just and peaceful society, ended up only by being accessible to top echelons of the clergy and of the laity in dioceses. The Commission therefore, against its wish, remained as elitist as it was before independence. The only change that occurred was the racial composition of the national executive which became more black than white.

Apart from the inhibitive political environment, one also notes that the conservative but powerful bishops and priests played no small role in the failure of the Commission to get down to the parishes and small Christian communities. The interests of the individual priests determined the amount of lay involvement in issues which had to do with justice and peace. Bishops and parish priests were crucial in all programmes of the Church, because they continued to direct the operations and life of the 'local Church'. The importance they attached to the CCJP's work, appears to have been very minimal as is shown by their disinterest in attending workshops and passing on information to the Parishioners. Instead of being facilitators, they often turned out to be stumbling blocks to the communication between the national diocesan offices, parishes and small Christian communities.

Furthermore, that the bishops only supported the Commission financially once in five years, and giving $200.00 per year, per diocese, clearly shows their lack of seriousness in weaning the Commission from overseas dependency. The odds are that the insistence of the Bishop's Conference that the Commission change its constitutional status from a lay organisation associating with the Bishops' Conference' to an Episcopal Commission, was an attempt to have direct control over its operations.

Overall, considering the short span of the period under study, and taking into account the inhibitions put in the Commission's way from both the Church and the State, the CCJP did sterling work. Its teachings on the rights and duties of citizens published in its newsletter, and its courageous comments on political problems that the country faced, showed a high level of commitment to justice and peace. And that the Church let the Commission play the role of advocate for justice and peace is a positive indicator of her prophetic responsibility to the society at large. Indeed it does represent a peak in the achievements of Zimbabwean Catholicism which was inspired by the vision and priorities from the new ecclesiology and social ethics of the Second Vatican Council.

## Notes

1. ZCBC Newsletter, No. 92, April 1980. This issue contains a special interview of the Prime Minister designate, Robert Mugabe, of 15 April 1980, carried out with the Ministry of Information, pp. 5–8.
2. Ibid. Cf. also Randolph, *Dawn in Zimbabwe*, pp. 40–41.
3. ZCBC *Newsletter, Independence Supplement*, 18 April 1980. The Supplement contained the statement of the Roman Catholic Bishops of Zimbabwe, dated 17 April 1980. The Statement extensively drew upon Vatican II teachings contained in *Gaudium et spes*, Nos. 42, 44, 76 and 78, pp. 9–11.

CHAPTER 7 — *Justice & Peace Commission in Independent Zimbabwe (1980–85)* 121

4. ZCBC Statement, 17 April, 1980, p.9.
5. *Ibid.*
6. *Ibid.*
7. *Ibid.*
8. *Ibid.*, p.10.
9. P Chakaipa, Prayer to bless the Zimbabwe flag, 17 April 1980. In ZCBC *Independence Supplement*, p.12.
10. *Ibid.*
11. Cf. note 1.
12. Independence Mass of Thanksgiving — 18 April 1980. In *Independence Supplement*, pp. 16–18. No account of the Mass was recorded in the Zimbabwe Media. There had been no public announcement of the Mass except within Church leadership circles. One Catholic overseas reporter, however, covered the mass in the Harare diocese' Catholic Cathedral.
13. *Ibid.*
14. *Ibid.*, p.16.
15. ZCBC *Newsletter*, No. 94, August, 1980, p.11.
16. Fr F Mukonori argues that this view was shared mainly by diocesan representatives, many of whom were diocesan *ex officio* members of the national executive. Interview, at Prestage House, on 28 September, 1988.
17. CCJP Minutes of the Annual General Meeting of the national executives, September 1980, p.2. In CCJP Harare Archives.
18. 'Programme 1982', p.2. CCJP blueprint for the future, February 1982. In CCJP Harare Archives.
19. Cf. note 17. Also Dept. of Information, President's Statement 563/80, 12 September 1980. (In Ministry of Information).
20. Minutes of the CCJP AGM, September 1980, p.12.
21. *Ibid.*
22. *Ibid.*
23. *Ibid.*
24. *Ibid.*
25. *Ibid.*, p.14.
26. *Ibid.*
27. ZCBC *Newsletter*, No 102, February 1992, p.4.
29. *Ibid.*
30. *Ibid.*
31. *Ibid.*

32. CCJP, Minutes of the Annual General Meeting held on 28 February 1982, p.2.
33. Ibid.
34. Preface to the new constitution of the Justice and peace Commission. Cf. ZCBC Newsletter, No. 102, February 1982 p.4.
35. Ibid. Cf. Objective three.
36. ZCBC Newsletter, No. 102, February 1982, p.4.
37. Ibid.
38. Ibid.
39. Ibid.
40. Fr F Mukonori (Formerly Brother Mukonori), Interview at Wadzanai Training Centre, 23 August 1993.
41. ZCBC Newsletter, No. 102, op.cit., p.4.
42. Ibid.
43. Ibid.
44. Ibid.
45. 'Programme 82', op.cit.
46. Ibid., p.3.
47. CCJP, Minutes of the Annual General Meeting held on 28 February, 1983, p.3.
48. Ibid.
49. This was expressed by the Chairman of the JPC in his vote of thanks to the Prime Minister, Robert Mugabe for his speech. Cf. Minutes of the Gwelo Seminar of 5–6 February 1982, p.2. In CCJP Harare Archdiocese Archives.
50. Comments made at the CCJP AGM of 28 February 1982. Cf. note 32. p.5.
51. ZCBC, minutes of the Plenary Session of IMBISA, held on 2 June 1980, p.5.
52. Ibid.
53. ZCBC Memo, in MS/RR/21/06/82 of the General Secretariat Archives, p.8.
54. Ibid., p.6.
55. Ibid.
56. Ibid.
57. Ibid.
58. CCJP, Minutes of the AGM of February 1983. Cf. note 47.
59. CCJP, Report on National Workshop, held from 20 to 23 August 1985, p.1.
60. CCJP Newsletter, No.5, June 1985, p.1.
61. Cf. Zimbabwe Constitution Order 1979, Chapter III, Declaration of Rights, para. 19.
62. CCJP workshop, Cf. note 59.

63. *Ibid.*
64. *Ibid.*
65. *The Herald*, 29 and 30 June 1985.
66. CCJP Workshop, Cf. note 59.
67. *Ibid.*, p.8.
68. *Ibid.*
69. *Ibid.*
70. *Ibid.*
71. *Ibid.*, p.11.
72. *Ibid.*, p.11.
73. *Ibid.*, p.14.
74. CCJP, Annual Report for the year 1983, p.4.
75. *Ibid.*
76. *Ibid.*
77. *Ibid.*
78. CCJP, Annual Report for 1982, p.6.
79. CCJP, Annual Report for 1983, p.4.
80. *Ibid.*
81. *Ibid.*
82. *Ibid.*
83. CCJP, Annual Report for 1984, .4. Also Annual Report for 1985, p.6. In CCJP Archives.
84. CCJP Annual Report for 1984.
85. CCJP Annual Report for 1985, p.6.
86. D Auret, *Reaching for Justice*, p.147.
87. *Ibid.*
88. *Ibid.*, p.144.
89. P Gundani, 'A study on Church and State in Zimbabwe — The Roman Catholic Church and State, 1980–1986', MA dissertation, UZ, February, 1987, pp. 118–175. D Auret, *op.cit.*, pp. 147–166. These two studies give a detailed exposition and analyses of the contribution of the CCJP to the dissident crisis in Matabeleland and Midlands provinces. See also R Werbner, *Tears of the Dead*, (1992), for the role of the Fifth Brigade in Matabeleland.
90. CCJP, Annual Report for 1983, p.5.
91. CCJP *Newsletter*, No. 4, November, 1984, p.1.
92. *Ibid.*

93. *Ibid.*, pp. 1-2
94. *The Herald*, 4 November 1984.
95. D Auret, *op.cit.*, pp. 159-165.
96. CCJP, Annual Report for 1985, p.5.
97. *Ibid.*
98. *Ibid.*, p.7.
99. *Parade Magazine*, February, 1985, p.1. See also CCJP, minutes of the Annual General Meeting in February 1985, p.7.
100. CCJP, Minutes of the Annual General Meeting, February, 1985, p.7.
101. *Ibid.*, p.6.
102. *Ibid.*
103. CCJP Newsletter, No. 5, June 1985, p.1.
104. *Ibid.*, p.2.
105. *Ibid.*
106. *Ibid.*
107. D Auret, *op.cit.*, p. 163.
108. These organisations are mentioned at the end of every annual report.
109. Chairman's report at a CCJP Meeting held on 30 September 1981.
110. *Ibid.*
111. Catholic Bishops' letter to the chairman of the CCJP cf. Appendix to minuts of the meeting held on 30 September, 1981.
112. Bishop P Mutume, President of the CCJP. Interview at the General Secretariat, on 15 March, 1990.
113. *Ibid.*
114. CCJP Annual Report, 1983, p.7.
115. *Ibid.*, p.8.
116. *Ibid.*
117. CCJP Annual Report, 1984, p.3.
118. CCJP Annual Report, 1985, p.2.

## Chapter 8

# Reflections

> There are a good many of faithful, well informed in many areas who, for the advantage of the Church have to be heard when issues come up in which they have some special competence which the clergy frequently lacks. (**Bishop of Manchester, Council Speeches of Vatican II**)

## Introduction

As we saw at the very beginning of this study, the perspective of the Second Vatican Council on the Church as the People of God, provides the foundation upon which both the laity and the clergy are called to co-responsible partnership with one another in Church and society. Theoretically, this new ecclesiological perspective was meant to bring about a change of thinking and relationships between the laity and clergy.

In practice, however, it has been difficult to translate the conciliar vision into practical relationship. The process of implementing the teachings of the Second Vatican Council have therefore been very gradual and to some extent contradictory in the case of the Church in Zimbabwe.

## The impetus for change

Attempts to transform pre-colonial organisations like the Catholic Association, proved quite difficult because of the top-down approach that the hierarchy used. The tensions and conflicts that raged between the Catholic National Council for the Laity that the Bishops' Conference had established, and the Catholic Association, were more than just pangs ushering the birth of a new Church. They were symptoms of the manner in which the hierarchy conducted their business in a Church which had a low view of the laity and where racial tension between black and white prevented any attempt at a creative synergy. The Catholic Association had not been properly consulted by the hierarchy on the transformation that the latter wanted to see in the Church. The Catholic Association were therefore resisting the hierarchy's top — down approach that they viewed as an imposition. This was true also for the CCJP.

Structures like the National Council of the laity, the Pastoral Council, Diocesan Council of the Laity and Parish Council were introduced in line with decisions adopted by the bishops and priests. The laity were not consulted prior to implementation stages. Gradually, however, they were able to adjust to, and make use of these innovations.

This approach was used in Salisbury diocese by Archbishop Markall, when he wanted lay teachers and the Catholic Association to play an influential role in the newly established local councils from 1971. The teachers accepted the change brought upon them by the State and the Church, two powerful institutions which were freeing the schools from their control. The change that came about empowered them to resist the extra responsibility that the hierarchy was imposing on them. As for the Catholic Association, the change being brought to bear on them by the hierarchy was viewed as supplanting the power base that its members operated from within the parish.

The impetus for change also tended to come about as a result of change of policies in Rome. This was the case on the need to stop training full-time catechists in the early 1970s. The call for self-support which in turn created the need for the development of small Christian communities founded on voluntary leaders, came from Rome. The same applies to the Justice and Peace Commission in 1972. The decision to form this new organ came about as a response to developments in Rome. Equally the change of stance that the CCJP adopted in 1978, was a result of the war which was swinging towards the Patriotic Front forces.

External factors had a definite impact on how the ecclesiological and socio-ethical signals from the Second Vatican Council were appropriated. Thus we saw that the Church's decision to hand over primary schools to local councils in response to new educational policies of the racialist minority regime forced the Church to develop a new pastoral strategy in line with the Council's teachings on small Christian communities. In the same way external pressures in the course of the war led the Church to translate its new insights in social ethics in terms of open and frank discussions with the leaders of the liberation movements.

## Power-sharing trends

From the teething problems of the late 1960's up to 1985, the process of power sharing has tended to follow racial and élitist lines. Let us examine these trends chronologically.

### *From 1965 to 1973*

The first period, that is from 1965 to 1973, was characterised by the trend to share power between the missionary clergy and the white members of the Church.

The new pastoral structures that were established during this period, were headed by members of the white elite in the Church. Such structures included the Catholic National council for the Laity, Catholic Social Services and Development and the Catholic Commission for Justice and Peace. Even the leadership structures in dioceses like Salisbury, Gwelo, and Bulawayo, where there were substantial white members, reflected this tendency. During this period, the few black elite who were sometimes co-opted to the executives of these organisations, only occupied the positions of committee members.

The racial tendency, prevalent in the power-sharing modes of this period can be explained historically. In a racist society that viewed blacks as second-class citizens, the norm was that in practice the Church would reflect the State of the society at large. Although the Church as such did not believe in racism, the belief may have been that meaningful change of mind leading to racial tolerance had to come form the whites themselves.

The hierarchy's dependence on the white elite, resulted in its failure to offer advice to the black members of the laity at the time of the Sir Douglas Home-Smith Internal Settlement in 1972. The Catholic Association had to resort to political stalwart Edison Sithole for advice. The dilemma that the hierarchy found itself in 1970 over the issue of the administration of the schools reflects the Church's deep-seated paternalism to the black people. The hierarchy, as teachers of the Church, had not learnt to listen to the black laity. Whatever implications the surrender of the schools in terms of Church-State relationships had, the bottom line is that the opinions of the black members of the Church were not solicited. Ultimately the black people had to pay the price of shouldering a heavier burden in educating their children.

## From 1974 to 1978

This period may be construed as the watershed that defined a new perception of power-sharing modes in the Church. The first evidence of this change came about when the indigenous diocesan clergy were given the recognition by the hierarchy, that they were the group upon which the success of liturgical developments rested. This new role of the indigenous diocesan clergy was consolidated through the consecration of Rev P F Chakaipa as Archbishop of Salisbury, and of Rev T Chiginya as Bishop of Gwelo, in 1976 and 1977 respectively. Although Rev P F Chakaipa had been ordained Auxiliary Bishop in 1973, he did not have the right to succession of Archbishop Markall. He was therefore just like a Vicar General, because he did not have administrative power of a co-adjutor Bishop.

However it is worth noting that it was during this period that the concept of the local Church and of the small Christian community was adopted in pastoral discourses. The local African character was therefore gradually coming into the Church. During the same period, the Justice and Peace Commission switched leadership from whites to blacks. It became more actively involved in the plight of the suffering Africans in the war-stricken areas of Zimbabwe. This led to the new relationships between the clergy and the laity on the local level as well as between the liberation movements and the Church on the national and international scene.

In this transitional period, especially towards its end, a black bishop like Archbishop Chakaipa, and a priest like Fr B Ndlovu, an African brother like F Mukonori and a laymen like I Muvingi were considered to be very crucial assets in as far as contacts with the guerrilla leaders were concerned. Contacts with the leaders of the Patriotic Front became very important from 1978, at a time that the Church was getting more and more concerned about its future role in a free Zimbabwe.

In spite of the changes that we have identified above, the relationship between the clergy and the ordinary laypersons did not change drastically. For instance, while the indigenous diocesan priests through the NADC were highly rated by both laity and clergy, they in turn did not seem to have changed the views of the laity.

The low view of the laity that the indigenous priests had, seems to have been a result of the recognition, that in spite of the new accent on the local leadership within the context of the small Christian communities, these communities had to depend on priests for their sacramental life. The community model adopted since 1974 retained an exaggerated role and self-importance of the ordained at the expense of the entire community of the baptised.

## *From 1979 to 1985*

The contact that the leadership of the Church made with the leadership of the Patriotic Front, boosted the confidence of the former concerning future co-operation with the Church in an independent Zimbabwe. Through the CCJP the Church continued to operate at the service of the people of Zimbabwe as the war came to a close in 1979.

After independence, the Church continued to underscore the principle that service, which incudes services in the socio-political order, is as constitutive to its mission as preaching of the word and sacramental celebration.

A problem remained in which the Church, through educated members, which had now taken over the running of this organisation, failed to make the ordinary Catholics within the small Christian community appreciate the importance of justice as part of their faith. Hence the CCJP failed to solicit financial support from within Zimbabwe. Notwithstanding the continued significance of the CCJP at the national and international socio-political levels, the organisation remained exclusively élitist in its approaches. Therefore the predominant image of the Catholic Church was still the 'Church for the people': it was not yet a 'Church of the people'.

## Ecclesiological implications

Throughout the period of study, it is possible to characterise the ecclesiological shifts that the Church underwent in terms of the three models. These are the institutional, the community and the servant models.

However, it is difficult to say that the church shifted form one distinct model to another. Rather, the process of transformation that occurred resulted in the existence of the three models side by side. In terms of power distribution, the institutional form of ecclesiology implies that power remained in the hands of the clergy. Meanwhile, the community ecclesiology entails power sharing between clergy and laity, together as people of God. However, an ecclesiology based on service, entails a recognition by the Church in its institutional and/or communitarian expressions to serve the society at large through programmes that help empower marginalised sectors out of domination. Such socially responsible affirmative action places the Church in a position to broker power between the dominating and dominated sectors of the society. This was the case with the CCJP which helped broker power between the white minority and the black majority in both Church and society at large. Nevertheless, by the end of 1985, when this study ended, the 'local church' as the real pivot in Zimbabwean Catholicism was yet to be realised. Establishing a self-supporting, self-propagating and self-ministering 'local church' remains a daunting challenge, as the Church struggles to thrust its roots deeper within the indigenous cultures of Zimbabwe.

## Sources

# Primary Sources

## 1. ORAL INTERVIEWS

### 1.1 Laypersons

| | |
|---|---|
| Mr A Banda | Boarding master, Mukaro Mission, 16 October 1992 |
| Mr P Chadya | Teacher, Mt. St Mary's, 28 October 1990 |
| Mrs Chidoori | Secretary, Murezi, Assisi parish, Chivhu, 22 May 1990 |
| Mr Chifamba | Member, New Church, St Peter's Parish, Harare, 1 April 1990 |
| Mr Chigwedere | Former Council Secretary, Chivhu, 17 June 1991 |
| Mr E Chikuvire | Teacher, Murezi, Assisi Parish, Chivhu, 14 August 1991 |
| Mrs T Chikuvire | Secretary, Murezi, Assisi Parish, Chivhu, 14 August 1991 |
| Mrs E Chinhengo | lay leader, Chiriga, Serima Parish, 16 June 1992 |
| Mr Chinhondo | Secretary, Gokomere Mission, 25 August 1991 |
| Mr Chinzuma | Member, New Church, St Peters Parish, Harare, 2 April 1990 |
| Mr P Chipanera | Mass Centre Chairman, Murezi, Assisi Parish, 28 December 1992 |
| Mrs Conradie | Secretary, Mabelreign Parish, Harare, 6 June 1990 |
| Mrs Davis | Member, St Martins Braeside Parish, Harare, 10 February 1990 |
| Mr E Doba | Teacher, Chivhu, 12 November 1992 |
| Mr Dunduru | Choir master, New Church, St Peter's Parish, Harare, 1 May 1990 |
| Mr Fierao | Chairman, Braeside Parish, 1 April 1990 |
| Mr D Geach | Chairman of Pastoral Council, 1968-72. Archdiocese of Salisbury, Waterfalls, St Francis Parish, 2 September 1990 |

# Sources

| | |
|---|---|
| Mrs Geach | Member, Waterfalls, St Francis Parish, Harare, 2 September 1990 |
| Mr Goredema | Member, New Church, St Peters Parish, Harare, 1 May 1990 |
| Mr Joseph | Lay leader, St Martins, Braeside Parish, Harare, 17 May 1990 |
| Mrs Kwaramba | Lay leader, Kambuzuma, Harare, 4 May 1990 |
| Mrs Kwedza | Chairperson of the Guild of the Lady of Heaven (Hosiyedenga), New Church, St Peters' Parish, 3 June 1990. |
| Mr Machorani | Chairman of Parish Council, Gokomere Parish, 25 August 1991. |
| Mrs Magaya | Mt St Mary's Parish, Wedza, 28 September 1991. |
| Mr Mahuni | Headmaster, Murezi Mass Centre, 20 September 1990. |
| Mr Makanyire | Member, Mukaro Mission, 26 November 1991. |
| Mrs Mamvura | Member, St Peter's Parish, Harare, 3 May 1990. |
| Mr E Matirongo | Student, University of Zimbabwe, 6 December, 1992. |
| Mr A Matura | Administrator, Muonde Hospital, Driefontein, Mvuma, (1986-92) |
| Mr Maturure | Member, Mukaro Parish, Gutu, 18 November 1990. |
| Mr L Mavhengere | Director, National Catholic Youth Council (NCYC), 24 March 1992. |
| Mr Moffat | Member, St Peter's Parish, Harare, 5 May 1990. |
| Mr V Mugwagwa | Student, University of Zimbabwe, 4 August, 1992. |
| Mr N Mukora | Member, St Francis Parish, Waterfalls, Harare, 16 August 1991. |
| Mrs O Mukora | Member, St Francis Parish, Waterfalls, Harare, 16 August 1991. |
| Mrs Murembeni | Member, New Church, St Peter's Parish, Harare, 2 May 1990. |
| Mr Murindagomo | Secretary, St Francis Parish, Waterfalls, Harare, 17 August 1991. |

| | |
|---|---|
| Mr S Mushandu | Leader of Wesleyan Congregation, Chivhu, 17 October 1991. |
| Mrs Mutsindikwa | Chairperson of Parish Council 1990–91, Assisi Mission Parish, Chivhu, 12 August 1991. |
| Mr G Nematadzira | Boardingmaster, Gokomere Parish, 28 September 1991. |
| Mr N Ndebele | Director of the Catholic Commission for Justice and Peace (1985–1991). Justice and Peace office, 10 July 1990. |
| Mr Ngwerume | Member, new Church, St Peter's Parish, Harare, 4 May 1990. |
| Mr Nyatsanza | Teaching Assistant, University of Zimbabwe, 19 September 1991. |
| Mr Nyazika | Member, St Peter's Parish, Harare, 5 May 1990. |
| Mrs Sanyangare | Member, St Peter's Parish, Harare, 5 May 1990. |
| Mr C Tome | Chairman of the Archdiocese's Pastoral Council, 1989–91, Headmaster of Mt St Mary's Secondary School 1980–1992, 26 September 1991. |
| Mrs Tome | Teacher, Mt St Mary's School, 26 September 1991. |
| Mrs Vhuta | Member, St Peter's New Church, 16 February 1992. |
| Mr Zata | Member, St Peter's New Church, 16 February 1992. |
| Mr T Zawaira | Member, Masvingo, 19 May 1991. |
| Mr Zenda | Member, St Peter's Parish, Harare, 5 May 1990. |

At Tafara parish I carried out group interviews, in April 1991.

Section 1 had 19 women

Section 2 had 26 women

Section 3 had 12 women

Section 4 had 41 women

Section 5a had 20 women

Section 6a had 19 women

Section 6b had 13 women

Total number of women who attended were 159.

## 1.2 Catechists

| | |
|---|---|
| Mr Chitagu | Majada, Mukaro Mission, Gutu 23 August 1993. |
| Mr Gidesi | Tafara Parish, 19 June 1990. |
| Mr Nzero | St Peter's Parish, Harare, 2 May 1990. |
| Mr Ravhai | St Peter's Parish, Harare, 2 May 1990. |

## 1.3 Sisters

| | |
|---|---|
| Sr Denise Osterhaus (RSHM) | Mabelreign Parish, wrote down response, 12 April 1991. |
| Sr Edigna Regenbogen (OP) | St Martins, Harare, 26 March 1990. |
| Sr Gemma Chifamba (LCBL) | Education Secretary (1986–1990), CCP Diocesan Organiser (1976–1980) 12 April, 3 July, 9 and 10 September 1990. |
| Sr Julian Mpofu (CPC) | Wadzanai Training Centre, 16 September 1992. |
| Sr Lioba Gana (LCBL) | Mt St Mary's, Wedza, 28 October 1991. |
| Sr Lucia Mutirwa (LCBL) | Wadzanai Training Centre, 14 September 1992. |
| Sr Ludo Theodora Ncube (CPS) | Wadzanai Training Centre, 12 September 1992. |
| Sr Martin Mutimbanyoka | (LCBL), Highfields, 5 May 1990. |
| Sr Stella Maris, (LCBL) | Nazareth House, 18 September 1992. |
| Sr Teresa Corby, (LCM) | Doctor at Mr St Mary's Mission Hospital, Wedza, 26 October 1991. |
| Sr Veronica Traquino (OP) | Wadzanai Training Centre, 26 September 1992. |

## 1.4 Brothers

| | |
|---|---|
| Br F Mukonori (now priest) (SJ) | Prestage House, 28 September 1988 and Wadzanai Training Centre, 12 August 1993. |
| Br L Manhobo (SPB) | Wadzanai Training Centre, 15 September 1993. |

## 1.5 Bishops and priests

| | |
|---|---|
| Fr Blackie D (CSSR) | *Mission, 14 February and 28 August 1991. |
| Fr Jakata T (dioc) | Gokomere Training Centre, 13 February 1990, and 25 September 1991. |
| Fr Johnson N (SJ) | Prestage House, UZ Chaplain, 14 August 1991. |
| Fr Kinna P (SJ) | St Peter's Parish, Harare, 15 June 1991. |
| Fr Machingauta B (dioc) | The Good Shephered Church, Chiredzi, 18 February 1990. |
| Fr Marimazhira (dioc) | Mashava, 15 November 1991. |
| Fr Mackenna L (SJ) | Braeside Church, Harare, 28 April 1990. |
| Fr Makaka P (SJ) | Braeside Church, Harare, 29 April 1990. |
| Bishop Mugadzi F | (Gweru diocese), RCBC Secretary (1987) Gen Secretariat, 29 November 1987. |
| Fr Makonese TI (dioc) | The Good Shepherd Church, Chiredzi, 13 February, 1990. |
| Fr Modekai G. (SJ) | Mabelreign, 12 October 1992. |
| Fr McEnhill G. (SJ) | St Peter's Parish, Harare, 07 May 1990. |
| Bishop Mutume P | (Mutare diocese), Secretary to RCBC, 1982-1992, 4 September 1988, 12 March 1990, 15 March 1990 etc. 29 October 1991. |
| Fr Nyatsanza W (dioc) | University of Zimbabwe, 17 August 1990. |
| Fr O'Donell H (OFM) | St Francis Church, Waterfalls, Harare, 14 June 1991. |
| Fr Randolph RH (SJ) | Prestage House, 15 and 22 September 1988. |
| Fr Regan C (OFM) | Mount St Mary's Wedza, 27 September 1990. |
| Fr Russel T (OFM) | Pastoral Centre, 25 October 1992. |
| Fr Slevin P (OFM) | Mount St Mary's Wedza, 27 September 1990. |
| Fr Spence K (SJ) | Prestage House, 29 August 1988. |
| Fr Wermter O (SJ) | Communications Secretary for ZCBC, Pastoral Centre, 13 May 1993. |

## 2. ARCHIVE MATERIAL

### 2.1 Gokomere Training Centre Archives (GA)
Files     Laity — 1–5 (General)
File      NADC and later ZADC
File      LSC (Lenten Sacrifice Committee)
File      Adaptation (Kurova guva)
File      Miscellaneous 1972–1978
File      *Kristo* magazine 1974–1979
File      *Guti* (not systematised)

### 2.2 National Archives Harare (NAH)
*MOTO* Newspaper, 1959–1974, 1980–1985
*Rhodesia Herald*, assorted

### 2.3 Harare Archdiocese Archives (HAA)
File      Lay Apostolate (General)
File      Pastoral Council
File      CCP (Christian Community Programme)
File      Catholic association
File      Roman Catholic National Council of the Laity (RCCL)

### 2.4 Jesuit Archives (JA)
Boxes    41, 124 and 308 Education/Church schools
Boxes    66 Nationalism and the Church, Kumbirai, 1963
Box      320, 322 Justice and Peace Commission
Box      324-25 RCBC/ZCBC Newsletter, 1970–1985
Box      375 Land Tenure Act/JPC campaign/Peace Commission
Box      390 RCBC: Solidarity with lamont
Box      408 Internal settlement
Box      422-425 Randolph's notes
Box      52 file 2 — the visit of Ralph tanner

## 2.5 Justice and Peace Archives (JPA)

File      Political
File      The Catholic Church
File      The Church and the new State
File      Justice and Peace Newsletter 1980–1985
File      Minutes of A.G.M's 1972–1985

## 2.6 RCBC/ZCBC Archives (RCBC)

File on Liturgy/*Kurova guva*

RCBC/ZCBC Minutes 1970–1985

File Mission activity of the Roman Catholic Church in Rhodesia, 1950–1970

Miscellaneous 1972–1982.

Pastoral letters: A call to Christians (5 June 1969) A crisis of conscience (17 March 1970)

RCBC Newsletters, August 1970 — December 1985.

## 2.7 Private Archive

Sr Janice McLaughlin on the Commission for Justice and Peace (1977–1980)

## 2.8 Church Documents and Pastoral letters

A call to Christians (1969)
A Crisis of Conscience (1970)
The Land Tenure Act and the Church (1970)
Minamato (1973)
Road to Peace (1978)

## 3. SECONDARY SOURCES

### 3.1 Published works

ABBOT, W (Ed.) *The Documents of the Second Vatican*, New Jersey, New Century Publishers, 1966.

ASTROW, A *Zimbabwe: A Revolution that Lost its Way*, London, Zed Press, 1983.

AURET, D *Reaching for Justice*, Gweru, Mambo Press, 1991.

# Sources

BEST, A G AND DE BLIJ, J. *African Survey*, New York, John Wiley and sons, 1977.

BOX, A *St. Peter's Harare*, Gweru, Mambo Press, 1976.

BOURDILLON, M F C (Ed.). *The Shona Peoples*, Gweru, Mambo Press, 1987.

BURROUGH, P J *Angels Unawares*, West Sussex, Churchman Publishing, 1988.

CROSS, F L *The Oxford Dictionary of the Christian Church*, London, Oxford University Press, 1957.

DACHS, A J (Ed.) *Christianity South of the Zambezi (vol I)*, Gwelo, Mambo Press, 1979.

DANIELS, G M *Drums of War*, New York, The Third Press Inc., 1974.

DULLES, A *Models of the Church*, New York, Seabury Press, 1974.

ELTON, G R *The Practice of History*, London, Fontana Paperbacks, 1967.

FLANNERY, A *Vatican Council II, the Conciliar and Post Conciliar Documents*, New York, Costello Publishing Co., 1987.

GALBRAITH, K J *The Anatomy of Power*, Boston, Houghton Miffin Co., 1983.

GALVIN, P *The Formation of the Christian Community in Rural Areas*, Gweru, Mambo Press, 1966.

GRANT, C G *The African Predicament in Rhodesia*, New York, 1973.

HALLENCREUTZ, C F AND MOYO A M, *Church and State in Zimbabwe*, Gweru, Mambo Press, 1988.

HASTINGS, A *Church and Mission in Modern Africa*, London, Burns and Oates, 1967.

HUELS, J M *The Faithful of Christ* (The New Canon Law for the Laity) Chicago, Franciscan Herald Press, 1983.

J P C PUBLICATIONS *The Man in the Middle* (1975)
        *Civil War in Rhodesia* (1976)
        *Rhodesia, The Propaganda War* (1977)
        *The Rhodesia Election Campaign* (1980)

KEE, A (Ed.). *Z A Reader in Political Theology*, London, Burns and Oates, 1967.

KILLEFF, C & P (eds.). *Shona Customs*, Gwelo, Mambo Press, 1970.

KUNG, H & CONGAR, Y (et al.), *Council Speeches of the Second Vatican*, New Jersey, Paulis Press, 1964.

LAMONT, D *Speech from the Dock*, Essex, Kevin Mayhew Publishers, 1977. (Introduced by Sheeby T & Sudworth, E).

LAW, D *Guns and Rain: Guerrillas and Spirit Mediums in Zimbabwe*, London, James Currey, 1985.

LIEBARD, O M *Clergy and Laity*, Wilmington, McGrath Publishing Co., 1978.

LINDEN, I *The Catholic Church and the Struggle for Zimbabwe*, London, Longman, 1980.

MAINELLI, V P (Compiler). *Social Justice*, Wilmington, McGrath Publishing Co., 1978.

McBRIEN, R *Catholicism*, Minneapolis, Winston Press, 1981.

McDONAGH, E *Demands of Simple Justice, A Study of the Church, Politics and Violence*, Dublin, Gill and McMillan, 1980.

McLAUGHLIN, J *On the Frontline: Catholic Missions in Zimbabwe's Liberation War*, Harare, Baobab Books, 1996.

MBITI, J S *African Religious and Philosophy*, London, Heinemann, 1982.

NIEDERBERGER, O *The African Clergy in the Catholic Church in Rhodesia*, Gwelo, Mambo Press, 1973.

RANDOLPH, R H *Church and State in Rhodesia: 1969–1971 A Catholic View*, Gwelo, Mambo Press, 1971.

— *Report to Rome*, Gwelo, Mambo Press, 1978.

— *Dawn in Zimbabwe*, Gweru, Mambo Press, 1985.

RCBC *The Land Tenure Act and the Church*, Gwelo, Mambo Press, 1970.

SKELTON, K *Bishop in Smith's Rhodesia*, Notes of a turbulent Octave 1962-70, Gweru, Mambo Press, 1985.

VERSTRAELEN, F J *An African Church in Transition, A Case Study on the Roman Catholic Church in Zambia*, Leiden, Inter-University Institute for Missiological and Ecumenical Research, 1975.

WERBNER, R *Tears of the Dead*, Harare, Baobab Books, 1992.

WILHEIM, A *Christ Among us: A Modern Presentation of the Catholic Faith*, New Jersey, Paulist Press, 1981.

## 3.2 Seminar Papers, theses and unpublished manuscripts

CALLAGHAN, E 'The Teaching of Religion', paper presented at the Southern African Seminar, Oxford, September, 1970.

EDWARDS, P 'Implications for the Church of recent developments in Rhodesia', paper presented at the Southern African Seminar, Oxford, September, (1970).

ELSNER, J 'The Missionary and Socio-Economic Action', paper presented at the Southern African Seminar, Oxford, September, 1970.

GUNDANI, P H 'Church — State in Zimbabwe: The Roman Catholic Church and development, 1972–1985', MA thesis, University of Zimbabwe, 1987.

MAXWELL J D 'A study of the Roman Catholic Church from Rhodesia to Zimbabwe 1959–86 University of Manchester, BA thesis 1986'.

MCLAUGHLIN, J 'The Catholic Church and Zimbabwe's war of liberation, 1972–1980', PhD thesis, University of Zimbabwe, 1991. (Quoted as it was before being revised, shortened and published as *On the Frontline*, Harare: Baobab Books, 1996.)

NYATSANZA, W 'A prophetic voice to rulers of Zimbabwe before and after Independence,' BA Hons, dissertation, University of Zimbabwe, 1990.

TURNER, A 'Church, State and Nationalism: The changing role of the Roman Catholic Church in Rhodesia 1959–1978' BA Thesis, Manchester, 1978.

WEEKS, N 'What is the local church? The role of the priest', paper presented at the Southern African Seminar, Oxford, Sept 1970 (Jesuit Archives)

ZHUWAWO, C 'An investigation of Vashawasha *kurova guva* ceremony and the Catholic teaching on the life after death', BA (Hons) thesis, University of Zimbabwe, 1990.

# Index

## Name Index

*Ad Clerum* 77
Alapont, Alexander 53
Alderson, C. 37
Auret, Diana 2, 3, 65, 83; Michael 103, 105

Banana, Canaan 98, 101; Janet 98
Best, Allen 35
Bethlehem Fathers 28
Bex, Antony 54, 55
Bourdillon, M.F.C. 2
Burgos Fathers 28
Burrough, John 30

Callaghan, E. 35
Cardijn, J. 12
Carmelite Fathers 28
Cassidy, Edward 106
Catholic African Association, The 21
*Catholic Church, The and Zimbabwe* 3 and *the Struggle for Zimbabwe* 1
*Catholic Herald* 98
Chifamba, Gemma 32
Chakaipa, Patrick, F. 52, 83, 84, 87, 98, 127
Charles, Prince 98
Chiginya, T. 127
Chirau, Jeremiah 82
*Church and State in Rhodesia* 3
*Civil War in Rhodesia* 81
Congar, Y. 12
Conway, Cardinal 44

Dachs, A.J. 1
*Dawn in Zimbabwe* 3
Deary, John 103

Dube, Mark 114
Dupuis, Arthur 89
Edwards, Paul 35, 37
Elsener, Joseph 22

Fide, Propaganda 18
Field, Winston 30
Fisher, L. 4

Galvin, Patrick 57
*Gaudium et Spes* 66, 107
Gopwe, 83
Graham, A.J.P. 72, 74
Gundani, P.H. 2
Haene, A. 23, 30-33 passim, 70, 73, 74
Hannan, Michael 22, 51, 52
*The Herald* 113
Home, Douglas 49, 127
Huss, Bernard 21
Hyacinth, Sr. 106

*Indemnity & Compensation Act (1975)* 80
*Irish Times* 80

Jakata, T. 4, 45

Kaunda, Kenneth 83

Lamont, D. 68, 73, 74, 80, 81, 82, 89, 103
Lavoie, 18, 19
Lewis, P. 4
Linden, I. 1, 33, 65
*London Times* 80

*Man in the Middle* 80
Marembo, 83
Marimazhira, Xavier 23

INDEX                                                                 141

Markall, Francis 19, 126
Maruza, Sylvester 74, 80
Maxwell, D.J. 1
McAuley Michael 14
McBrien, 6
McLaughlin, Janice 1, 2, 4, 65, 82, 86, 88
McLoughlin, T.O. 78
Mhondoro, Clement 103
Milingo, I. 83
Mnangagwa, Emmerson 86
Mpisaunga, Etherton 80
Mugabe, Robert 86-88 passim, 96-99 passim, 106, 107
Mukonori, Fidelis 83, 89
Munodawafa, 83
Mutume, Patrick 4, 103
Muvingi, Ishmael 83
Muzenda, Simon 86
Muzorewa, Abel 82, 84, 89

Ndlovu, Bernard 83
Nkomo, Joshua 83-87 passim, 117; Stephen 83

O'Hea, Jerry 98
Octogesima Adveniens 66

Page, Tim 99
Parade Magazine 114
Paul, Vincent de 52
Pope Paul IV 67, 68; VI 70, 91

Populorum Progressio 66
Prieto, I. 76

Randolph, Richard, H. 1, 3, 27, 29, 103
Ranger, T.O. 2
Rea, W. Francis 1, 74-75
Reckter, Monsignor Helmut 83, 89
Reaching for Justice 2
Report to Rome 3
Rhodesia Catholic Bishops Conference Newsletter 28
Rhodesia: The Propaganda War 82

Sheehy, T. 81
Silundika, George 83
Sithole, Edison 49
Sithole, Ndabaningi 82
Skelton, Kenneth 31
Smith, Ian Douglas 27, 31, 49, 58, 82, 88, 127
Smulders, Wim 53, 54
Stewart, John 103
Sudworth, Eileen 81

Tanner, R. 35, 36
Tekere, Edgar 86
Tongogara, Josiah 86
Tredgold, Robert 80
Turner, A. 1, 2

Weeks, N. 38

## Subject Index

Armed struggle
    Church role, in 1, 2

Call for day of peace 67-68
Catechist
    training 43-50
Catholic
    African

Association 2, 4, 21, 23, 42, 47, 48, 58, 65, 70, 125, 127; Union 21, 24
Aims, of 21; archdiocese of Salisbury 23-24, 35, 49, 50; Bulawayo diocese 24; conflicts, in 23; Gwelo diocese 23, 77-78; inactivity, of 51;

missionary relations, with 50; Umtali diocese 24, 79; Wankie diocese 24;
Bishops Conference 3
Church
  ecclesiological shifts, in 129; election, and 114-116; human rights, and 66-67; liberation war, and 128; post-independence, state and 114-120; power sharing, in 126; programmes in Zimbabwe 3; racism, in 127
Commission for Peace and Justice 2, 6, 65
  Elections and 114-116; liberation war, and 128; Matebeleland disturbances, and 112; newsletter 111-116 *passim*; problems, in 111 see also Justice and Peace Commission;
Institute for International Relations 2; population 28, 45; priest population ratio 38; shortage, of 53
Fund for International Development 117, 118; National Council 125, 127
primary schools
  enrolment, in 28, 36; importance, of 34, 43
Central
  Agency for Joint Financing Development Programmes 117; Intelligence Organisation 114
Chishawasha Regional Seminary in Zimbabwe 14, 45
Church run schools
  advantages, of 37-38; disadvantages, of 36-37; number, of 28; influence on the youth 29-30; state conflict, with 36
  System 27-29
  advantages, of 34; contradictions, of 34, 35; expansion, of 28
Clergy, laity ratio 45
Commission
  on Catechetics 17, 57; for Social services and Development 100, 102, 104
Conference of Major
  Religious Superiors 47; Women Religious 47

Driefontein National Pastoral Consultation 56

Election violence
  Catholic Commission for Peace and Justice, on 113
Evangelisation 53
  of Peoples in Rome 43

Gokomere Training Centre 4, 56

Indemnity and Compensation Act (1975) 80

Justice and Peace Commission 4, 69-99
  black diocesan representatives, in 72-75; constitution, new 118; evaluation of operations, of 77-79; financial state, of 117-120; history, of 70-75; objectives, of 72; internal settlement, and 82-83; liberation war, and 79-82
  meetings, with
    ZANU 86-89; ZAPU 83-86

Lancaster House Constitution 99
Land
  Apportionment Act (1931) 30; Tenure Act (1969) 30, 33, 79
The Lavoie Survey 18-19
The Lusaka Commonwealth Heads of Government meeting 89

Mambo Press 4
Matebeleland disturbances 112-113

# INDEX

*Moto Magazine* 4

National
  Association for Diocesan Clergy 4, 128
  Catechetical School 43, 45-47
    enrolment, 45; graduates, from 45
  Council of the Laity 20-21
Native Councils Act (1957) 30
New
  Education bill (1969) 27
  policy
    Catholic Church reaction, to 29-33; Heads of Denominations, and 30-33; implications, of 30

*Parade Magazine* 114
Pariah
  conflicts, in 42; Councils 14, 16-17, 20, 21; definition, of 11-12;
Pastoral Councils 13-14
Patriotic Front 89, 128
  Zimbabwe African Peoples Union 114-116
Peters, St.
  Programme 54-56; success, of 55

Rhodesia
  Catholic Bishops Conference 4, 16-17, 27, 43, 44, 46, 66, 68, 70, 72, 73, 82, 90; Front Community Development programme 30
Right of Entry 46-49 *passim*
Roman Catholic

Church 1
  Institutional model 11
  Rhodesia 1, Zimbabwe 1, 5, 6
  Church missions 27, Council for the Laity 19, 20, 22

Tribal Trust Lands 29

Unilateral Declaration of Independence 7, 31

Vatican Council 3, 6, 11-17, 25, 29, 42, 48, 58, 65, 70, 91, 119, 125, 126
  Second
    emphasis, of 12, 13
  Third 17

Welfare Organisations Act (1966) 22

Zimbabwe
  African National
    Catholic Bishops Conference 4, 96-99, 107
    Liberation Army 89
    Peoples Revolutionary Army, clashes, with 112
  Union-PF 99, 114-116;
    Catholic Bishops Conference 4, 96-99
  Youth League 108

www.ingramcontent.com/pod-product-compliance
Lightning Source LLC
Chambersburg PA
CBHW021409290426
44108CB00010B/448